DICKINSON COLLEGE COMMENTARIES

General Editors

Christopher Francese
Asbury J. Clarke Professor of Classical Studies, Dickinson College

Bret Mulligan
Associate Professor of Classics, Haverford College

Eric Casey
Latin Teacher, Trinity School, New York City

Ariana Traill
Associate Professor of Classics, University of Illinois at Urbana-Champaign

John Gruber-Miller
Edwin R. and Mary E. Mason Professor of Languages, Cornell College

———•———

Dickinson College Commentaries publishes peer-reviewed annotated editions for readers of Latin and Ancient Greek. The series exists in both print and digital forms and aims to be responsive to the needs of readers, teachers, and students. Along with annotated editions DCC publishes Ancient Greek and Latin grammars and vocabularies, including the *Core Latin and Ancient Greek Vocabularies,* and running non-core vocabularies on each text. The online commentaries incorporate audio recordings, video elements, annotated images, and interactive and static maps. The series is supported by the Roberts Fund for Classical Studies at Dickinson College.

Core
Latin and Ancient Greek
Vocabularies

Christopher Francese
Asbury J. Clarke Professor of Classical Studies, Dickinson College

Dickinson College Commentaries
Dickinson College
Carlisle, Pennsylvania

Copyright © 2020, Christopher Francese

ISBN 978-1-947822-06-1

Dickinson College Commentaries 2020
www.dcc.dickinson.edu

Cover image: *Glass garland bowl*. C. late 1st century B.C. The Metropolitan Museum of Art, New
York. Edward C. Moore Collection, Bequest of Edward C. Moore, 1891. *Met Museum*. https://
www.metmuseum.org/art/collection/search/245787.

Table of Contents

The Dickinson College Commentaries Core Latin and Ancient Greek Vocabularies represent the most common words in Latin and Ancient Greek, based on large hand-analyzed data sets. The Latin list has roughly a thousand headwords or lemmas, the Greek five hundred. These account for approximately 70–80% of the word forms found in a typical text, excluding proper names. For Caesar's *Gallic War*, the figure is 91%; for Vergil's *Aeneid*, 81%. In Greek, 66% of the words in Sophocles' *Antigone* are in the DCC core, while the figure for Plato's *Euthyphro* is 82%. The words appear sorted in two ways, alphabetically and by frequency.

The lists were developed in 2012 at Dickinson College and are freely available online at Dickinson College Commentaries (dcc.dickinson.edu). This version is the same as the online one and is intended for the convenience of those who would prefer to have a physical copy. The online version also includes definitions in various modern languages besides English, as well as the option to sort by semantic group.

Sources of frequency data for the Latin core list

1. L. Delatte, Et. Evrard, S. Govaerts and J. Denooz, *Dictionnaire fréquentiel et index inverse de la langue latine* (Liège: Laboratoire d'Analyse Statistique des Langues Anciennes [LASLA], 1981). The *Dictionnaire fréquentiel* used a database of 794,662 word forms (582,411 from prose authors, 212,251 from poetry), grouped into 13,077 separate lemmas. The texts used include many golden age and canonical authors, such as Catullus, Caesar, some speeches of Cicero, Horace's *Odes*, Juvenal, Tacitus, Seneca, Vergil, Ovid, Tibullus, along with some less commonly read authors such as Persius, Quintus Curtius, and Vitruvius.

2. Paul B. Diederich "The Frequency of Latin Words and Their Endings" (Dissertation, University of Chicago, 1939), as digitized by Carolus Raeticus in 2011. Diederich used a database of 202,158 word forms (194,378 without proper names) from more than 200 authors "from Ennius to Erasmus," who appear in the *Oxford Book of Latin Verse*, *Avery's Latin Prose Literature*, and Beeson's *Primer of Medieval Latin*. His explicit goal was to provide readers with vocabulary going beyond the canonical school texts (like Vergil, Cicero, and Caesar) that Lodge (1922) and others relied on. His final tabulation included the number of times a given word occurred in classical prose, poetry, and medieval Latin, and all three together.

3. In an effort to include a wide chronological spectrum of Latin, I constructed a list of post-classical authors from the Perseus Digital Library and used the top thousand lemmas from that sample as a check on the more classically oriented lists of Diederich and LASLA. This sample

included authors such as Ammianus Marcellinus, Apuleius, Ausonius, The Venerable Bede, Boccaccio, Boethius, Claudian, St. Jerome, Christoforo Landino, Minucius Felix, Petrarch, Poliziano, Prudentius, the *Scriptores Historiae Augustae*, and Marco Girolamo Vida. The main contribution of this sample was to show the importance of certain words in Christian Latin, such as *dominicus, episcopus*, or *monasterium*, which were not prominent in the other lists. Since most of these are easily recognizable from English cognates, they were not included here. The Perseus post-classical sample also helped to make decisions in cases where Diederich and the LASLA list differed.

Definitions and quantities were adapted from various sources, including Lodge 1922, and the *Oxford Latin Dictionary*. The frequency rankings are derived from LASLA, and do not take Diederich's counts into consideration.

Sources of frequency data for the Greek core list

1. A subset of the comprehensive *Thesaurus Linguae Graecae* (TLG) database, frequency data kindly provided by Maria Pantelia of TLG. The subset included all texts in the database up to 200 CE, for a total of 20.003 million words; of this total, the period 100–200 CE accounts for about half, 10.235 million. The point of the chronological limit of 200 CE was to minimize any possible distortions that would be caused by the large amount of later Christian and Byzantine Greek in the TLG, texts that are not typically read by most students of ancient Greek. I would like to express my warm thanks to Prof. Pantelia for providing this valuable data. The TLG texts were analyzed automatically by the TLG's lemmatizer tool, which attempts to determine from what lemma or dictionary headword a given form derives. The lemmas were then ranked by frequency (ὁ, αὐτός, καί, δέ, and τίς coming in as the top 5, for example, with ὁ, i.e. the definite article, at 3,280,309 instances). The lemmatizer tool, however, is far from perfect, and considerable editing of the raw results was necessary to catch "rogue" words that rose high because they share a form or forms with an extremely common word. The adjective ἥμερος ("tame"), for example, is relatively rare, but its rank is inflated in the raw data because it shares some forms with the very common noun ἡμέρα ("day"). Confronted with an ambiguous form, the lemmatizer splits the occurrences of that form equally between the two (or more) possible lemmas, resulting in the promotion of some rarer lemmas, and the relative demotion of commoner ones. Some of those problems are easy to spot, but many are not.

2. The corpus of Greek authors at Perseus under PhiloLogic, which at the time our list was developed (summer 2012) contained approximately 5,000,000 words. This frequency data was kindly provided by Prof. Helma Dik of the University of Chicago. I would like to express my heartfelt thanks to Prof. Dik for providing this valuable data, and for her very

helpful advice about the list and related matters. Although the TLG data set is larger, the PhiloLogic frequency data is superior in that its Greek lemmatizer tool has been significantly improved by the intervention of humans who disambiguated some ambiguous forms. The number of disambiguated words in the PhiloLogic Greek corpus at the time of the creation of our list was over 360,000, including all of Homer, Hesiod, and Aeschylus, and several thousand-word samples from the rest of the corpus. For some authors, such as Lysias and Plato, the sample figure was closer to 12,000.

Differences in the lemmatizer tools and differences in the samples being analyzed led to considerable disagreement between the two "top 500" lists, the TLG list and the PhiloLogic list. Another complicating factor had to do with lemmatization, that is, the process of deciding what exactly counts as a dictionary headword in ancient Greek. Common words treated as a lemma by TLG but not by PhiloLogic include εἶδον and εἶπον; words treated as a lemma by PhiloLogic but not by TLG include εἰκός and ἔξεστι. A lemma like ἄκρος, while not in the top 500 in its own right based on the TLG data, might be included if the figures for the adverb ἄκρον, lemmatized separately by the TLG, were added.

In making the innumerable judgment calls of this type it was enormously helpful to have figures from two different samples. Where they agreed, we could accept the results with some confidence; where they disagreed, we could investigate the details in the TLG corpus itself and decide. A word like κίνησις, for example, rises very high in the TLG, but not in PhiloLogic. On further examination in the TLG corpus it emerges as very important in Aristotle and certain other philosophical texts, but not terribly common elsewhere. It was therefore omitted. παρασκευάζω fails to make the cut in the TLG but does in PhiloLogic. It turns out to be very common in classical prose, and so we kept it. Such examples could be multiplied. In doubtful cases, we preferred words common in classical Greek across genres, and tried to avoid words not extremely common in the standard authors, but whose frequency data was inflated due to being very common in specialized mathematical, medical, or Aristotelian texts. ψυχρός is an example of a word that makes the top 500 in TLG thanks to its prominence in medical texts (and was thus omitted here); the statistical prominence of γωνία is due to its appearance in very repetitive mathematical texts, and it was thus also rejected.

Occasional editing was also done to avoid the appearance of many words based on the same root. φιλία, included in PhiloLogic's top 500, was omitted here, since we already have the adjective φίλος. δικάστης, a possible candidate, was rejected because we already had δίκαιος and δίκη. A few words that didn't quite make the cut statistically were included because of their cultural importance, such as ἐλεύθερος and δαίμων. Some verbs whose simplex forms do not rise to the level of the top 500 on their own were included because they are extremely common as compounds of similar meaning: βαίνω and ἀγγέλλω, for instance. In general, compound verbs were only included in addition to the simplex forms when the compounds either a) were extremely common on their own, b) had a substantially different definition from the simplex, or c) were vastly more common than the simplex so that the simplex itself could be omitted. Thus παρασκευάζω but not σκευάζω.

The goal throughout was to achieve a balance between the goals of (unrealizable) statistical perfection on the one hand, and pedagogical utility on the other.

Definitions are intended to cover most or all of the principal meanings. Definitions were adapted from various sources, including Major 2008, Liddell and Scott's *Intermediate Greek-English Lexicon*, Logeion, and Harper and Wallace 1893.

The Bridge at Haverford College is a tool for the creation of custom, personalized, accurate vocabulary lists for a wide variety of Latin and Greek texts and textbooks. It uses hand-parsed texts from LASLA and elsewhere. Among other things, it can generate lists with the DCC core items excluded, so that once this core has been mastered more unusual words will be readily available without recourse to a dictionary.

Acknowledgments
For both lists many judgment calls had to be made about which words to include and how to list them. This work was carried out in 2012–13 with valuable help from the following:

- Prof. Maria Pantelia of the University of California Irvine, Director of Thesaurus Linguae Graecae (TLG), provided Greek frequency data

- Prof. Helma Dik of The University of Chicago, Director of Perseus under PhiloLogic and Logeion, provided Greek frequency data and much helpful advice

- Prof. Wilfred Major of Louisiana State University was of enormous help at an early stage of the development of the Greek list, especially in analyzing the TLG frequency data and spotting innumerable pitfalls in it.

- Dr. Eric Casey of Trinity School, New York City, proofread the Greek list at a later stage and is responsible for a great many improvements.

- Professors Meghan Reedy and Marc Mastangelo, both of Dickinson College, improved the Latin and the Greek lists by helping to decide which words to include and how to list them.

- Dickinson students Alice Ettling, James Martin, Meredith Wilson, and

Lara Frymark edited and proofread the lists in the summer of 2012, and created the semantic groupings and part of speech lists, which are available on the online version. They also helped compare the TLG and PhiloLogic Greek data, and digitized the LASLA Latin frequency data.

- Lara Frymark and Dickinson student Qingyu Wang created the searchable database versions in Drupal in the summer 2013 with help from Dickinson's web developer Ryan Burke.

- Alex Lee, a graduate student at the University of Chicago, improved both lists with his careful proofreading.

- The Greek principal parts are based partly on the lists of Evan Hayes and Stephen Nimis in their edition of Lucian's *True Story*, though I also consulted the TLG itself to determine which principal parts were actually in common use.

- Latin Instructor Ann Heermans-Booth and Prof. Scott Farrington of Dickinson made several valuable improvements to the Latin and Greek lists, respectively.

- Krista Hanley did excellent work formatting the lists to make them attractive and readable in printed form.

I am most grateful for the contributions of all these individuals. The lists would have been far poorer without their help. I take full responsibility for all remaining errors and infelicities and would be grateful to be notified of any you discover.

Christopher Francese, July 3, 2020

References

Crane, G. 1992–2020. *Perseus Digital Library*. Tufts University. http://www.perseus.tufts.edu/hopper/

Delatte, L., Et. Evrard, S. Govaerts and J. Denooz. 1981. *Dictionnaire fréquentiel et index inverse de la langue latine*. Liège: Laboratoire d'Analyse Statistique des Langues Anciennes.

Diederich, P.B. 1939. *The Frequency of Latin Words and Their Endings* (Dissertation). Chicago: The University of Chicago.

Dik, H. 2009–2018. *Perseus Under PhiloLogic*. University of Chicago. http://perseus.uchicago.edu/

_____. 2011–2020. *Logeion*. University of Chicago. https://logeion.uchicago.edu

Glare, P.G.W. 1982. *Oxford Latin Dictionary*. Oxford: Clarendon Press.

Harper, W.R. and J. Wallace. 1893. *Xenophon's Anabasis: Seven Books*. New York: American Book Co.

Hayes, E. and S. Nimis. 2014. *Lucian's A True Story: An Intermediate Greek Reader*. Oxford, OH: Faenum Publishing.

Liddell, H.G. and R. Scott. 1889. *An Intermediate Greek-English Lexicon*. Oxford: Clarendon Press.

Lodge, G. 1922. *The Vocabulary of High School Latin*. New York: Teachers College Columbia University.

Major, W. E. 2008. "It's Not the Size, It's the Frequency: The Value of Using a Core Vocabulary in Beginning and Intermediate Greek." *CPL Online* 4.1: 1–24. https://camws.org/cpl/cplonline/files/Majorcplonline.pdf

Muccigrosso, J. 2004. "Frequent Vocabulary in Latin Instruction." *Classical World* 97: 409–433.

Mulligan, B. 2014–2020. *The Bridge*. https://bridge.haverford.edu/

Pantelia, M. 2001–2020. *Thesaurus Linguae Graecae*. http://stephanus.tlg.uci.edu

LATIN

A

ā ab abs	from, by (+abl.)
abeō -īre -iī -itum	go away
absum abesse āfuī	be away, absent
ac	and in addition, and also, and; (after comparatives) than; simul ac, as soon as; → atque
accēdō -cēdere -cessī -cessum	approach
accidō -cidere -cidī	fall; happen
accipiō -cipere -cēpī -ceptum	receive
ācer ācris ācre	sharp, piercing
aciēs -ēī f.	edge; line of battle
ad	to, up to, towards (+acc.)
addō -dere -didī -ditum	give to
addūcō -ere -dūxī -ductum	lead to, induce
adeō	(adv.) to such a degree, so
adeō -īre -iī -itum	go to
adhibeō -hibēre -hibuī -hibitum	apply
adhūc	thus far, to this point
adsum adesse affuī	be present
adveniō -īre -vēnī -ventum	come to, arrive at
adversus -a -um	facing, opposed; unfavorable
adversus (-um)	(adv. and prep.) facing, opposite, against, opposed (to)
advertō -vertere -vertī -versum	turn towards
aedēs -is f.	building; (pl.) house

aeger aegra aegrum	sick
aegrē	with difficulty
aequē	equally
aequor aequoris n.	level surface, sea, plain
aequus -a -um	equal
āēr āeris m.	air
aes aeris n.	copper, bronze
aetās -tātis f.	age, time of life
aeternus -a -um	everlasting, eternal
aethēr aetheris n.	pure upper air, ether, heaven, sky
aevum -ī n.	eternity; lifetime, age
afferō afferre attulī allātum	bring to
afficiō -ficere -fēcī -fectum	affect, visit with (+ abl.)
ager agrī m.	field
agitō -āre	drive
āgmen -minis n.	line of march
agō agere ēgī āctum	drive, do, act
aiō	say, affirm, say yes; ut āiunt: as they say
albus -a -um	white
aliēnus -a -um	foreign, strange
aliquandō	at some time, at length
aliquis -quae -quod	some, any; si quis, si quid: anyone who, anything that
aliter	otherwise, differently

alius -a -ud	other, another; ālias: at another time
alō alere aluī alitum	nourish
alter altera alterum	other of two
altus -a -um	high, lofty; deep
amīcitia -ae f.	friendship
amīcus -a -um	friendly; (as subst.) friend
āmittō -mittere -mīsī -missum	let go, send away
amnis -is m.	river, torrent
amō -āre	to love; amāns -ntis m./f.: lover
amor -ōris m.	love
amplus -a -um	large, spacious
an	or (in questions); utrum ... an: whether ... or
anima -ae f.	breath, spirit
animal -ālis n.	a living being, an animal
animus -ī m.	spirit, mind
annus -ī m.	year
ante	before, in front of (adv. and prep. + acc.)
antequam	before
antīquus -a -um	ancient, old-time, former
aperiō aperīre aperuī apertum	open
appāreō -ēre -uī	appear, become visible
appellō -pellāre	call, address, name
aptus -a -um	fit, suitable

apud	near, in the presence of (+acc.)
aqua -ae f.	water
āra -ae f.	altar
arbitror arbitrārī arbitrātus sum	consider, think
arbor arboris f.	tree
ārdeō ārdēre ārsī ārsum	blaze, glow; be eager
argentum -ī n.	silver, money
arma -ōrum n. pl.	arms, weapons
ars artis f.	skill
arvum -ī n.	ploughed land, field
arx arcis f.	citadel, castle; summit
ascendō -ere -scendī -scēnsum	climb up, ascend
aspiciō -ere -spēxī -spectum	look to or at, behold
astrum -ī n.	star; constellation
at	but, but yet
atque	and in addition, and also, and; (after comparatives) than; simul atque, as soon as; → ac
auctor -ōris m.	originator, founder
auctōritās -ātis f.	influence, clout, authority
audāx audācis	bold, daring; reckless
audeō audēre ausus sum	dare, be eager
audiō -īre -īvī/-iī -ītum	hear, listen to
auferō auferre abstulī ablātum	take away
augeō augēre auxī auctum	increase

aura -ae f.	breeze
aureus -a -um	golden; splendid
auris -is f.	ear
aurum -ī n.	gold
aut	or
autem	moreover, but, however
auxilium -ī n.	support, assistance; (pl.) auxiliary forces
avis -is f.	bird

B

barbarus -ī m.	foreigner, barbarian
beātus -a -um	happy, blessed, prosperous, fortunate
bellum -ī n.	war
bene	well
beneficium -ī n.	service, kindness
bonus -a -um	good
bōs bovis m.	ox; gen. pl. boum
brevis -e	short, shallow, brief
breviter	briefly

C

cadō cadere cecidī cāsum	fall, be killed
caecus -a -um	blind, unseeing; dark, obscure
caedēs -is f.	killing, slaughter
caedō caedere cecīdī caesum	strike, kill, cut down
caelestis -e	from or of heaven; caelestēs, the gods
caelum -ī n.	sky, heavens
campus -ī m.	plain, field
candidus -a -um	white, fair
canis -is m./f.	dog
canō canere cecinī cantum	sing
capiō capere cēpī captum	seize
caput capitis n.	head
careō -ēre -uī	lack (+ abl.)
carmen -inis n.	song
cārus -a -um	dear
castrum -ī n.	fortress, (regularly plural, castra camp)
castus -a -um	pure, spotless, chaste
cāsus -ūs m.	a fall; chance, accident
causa -ae f.	cause, reason; causā + preceding genitive, for the sake of
caveō cavēre cāvī cautum	be on guard, beware
cēdō cēdere cessī cessum	go, move; yield
celebrō -āre	frequent, throng, crowd

celer -is -e	swift
celeriter	quickly
cēnseō cēnsēre cēnsuī cēnsum	assess, rate; think, decide
centum	one hundred
cernō cernere crēvī crētum	discern, separate
certē	certainly, surely
certō -āre	decide by contest; fight, compete, vie
certus -a -um	sure, fixed
cēterum	for the rest, in addition, however that may be
cēterus -a -um	the others, the rest
cibus -ī m.	food
cingō cingere cīnxī cīnctum	encircle, surround, gird
cinis cineris m./f.	ashes, embers
circā	around (adv. and prep. +acc.)
citus -a -um	swift; citō swiftly
cīvis -is m./f.	citizen
cīvitās -ātis f.	citizenship, state
clāmor -ōris m.	outcry, shout
clārus -a -um	clear, distinguished
classis -is f.	class, division, fleet
claudō claudere clausī clausum	close, shut
coepī coepisse coeptus	begin
cōgitō -āre	think, reflect

cōgnōscō -gnōscere -gnōvī -gnitum	learn, understand
cōgō cōgere coēgī coāctum	drive together; compel
cohors cohortis f.	cohort, band, troop
colligō -ere -lēgī -lēctum	gather together, collect
colō colere coluī cultum	inhabit, cultivate
color -ōris m.	color
coma -ae f.	hair, tresses
comes comitis m./f.	companion, comrade; attendant, follower
committō -mittere -mīsī -missum	join, entrust to (+dat); perform, do
commūnis -e	common, general
comparō -āre	get ready, provide; compare
compōnō -pōnere posuī positum	build, construct, arrange
concēdō -cēdere -cessī -cessum	yield, withdraw
condīciō -ōnis f.	agreement, condition
condō -dere -didī -ditum	build, found; store up; hide, conceal
cōnferō cōnferre contulī collātum	collect, bring to
cōnficiō -ficere -fēcī -fectum	complete, accomplish; destroy, kill, consume
cōnfiteor cōnfitērī cōnfessus sum	admit (a fact), confess (a crime); reveal, disclose
coniunx coniugis m./f.	spouse, husband, wife
cōnor cōnārī cōnātus sum	try, attempt
cōnsequor -sequī -secūtus sum	follow up, overtake, attain
cōnsilium -ī n.	plan; council, group of advisors

cōnsistō -sistere -stitī	take position; consist in, be composed of
cōnstituō -stituere -stituī -stitūtum	establish, put together
cōnstō -stāre -stitī	agree; constat, it is established that (+ acc. and infin.)
cōnsuētūdo -inis f.	custom, habit
cōnsul -ulis m.	consul
cōnsulō -sulere -suluī -sultum	consult, plan (+ acc.); consider the interests of (+ dat.)
cōnsūmō -sūmere -sūmpsī -sūmptum	to use up, consume
contemnō -temnere -tempsī -temptum	despise, scorn, disdain
contineō -tinēre -tinuī -tentum	contain, restrain
contingō -tingere -tigī -tactum	touch, be contiguous to
contrā	against, opposite (adv. and prep. +acc.)
conveniō -venīre -vēnī -ventum	assemble, meet; agree
convertō -vertere -vertī -versum	turn about, turn, change
convīvium -iī n.	banquet, feast
cōpia -ae f.	abundance; (pl.) troops
cor cordis n.	heart; cordī est, it is pleasing to (+ dat.)
cornu -ūs n.	horn
corpus corporis n.	body
corrumpō -rumpere -rūpī -ruptum	break up, destroy, ruin
crēdō crēdere crēdidī crēditum	believe
creō -āre	produce, create; elect, choose
crēscō crēscere crēvī crētum	grow, increase

crīmen -inis n.	verdict, accusation
culpa -ae f.	guilt, fault, blame
cum	with (prep. + abl.); when, since, although (conjunction + subj.)
cūnctus -a -um	entire all together
cupīdō -inis f.	desire, eagerness, craving
cupiō -ere -īvī -ītum	desire
cūr	why?
cūra -ae f.	care, concern
cūrō -āre	watch over, look after, care for (+ acc.)
currō currere cucurrī cursum	run
currus -ūs m.	chariot
cursus -ūs m.	course, advance
custōs custōdis m.	guardian

D

damnō -āre	condemn
damnum -ī n.	damage, injury
dē	down from, about, concerning (+ abl.)
dēbeō dēbēre dēbuī dēbitum	owe, be obliged
decem	ten
dēcernō -cernere -crēvī -crētum	determine, decide
decet decēre decuīt	it is right, proper, fitting (+ acc. + infin.)

LATIN: Alphabetic Listing

decus decoris n.	beauty, grace; ornament, glory, honor
dēdūcō -dūcere -dūxī -ductum	launch, lead away
dēfendō -fendere -fendī -fēnsum	defend, ward off
dēferō -ferre -tulī -lātum	carry away, report
deficiō -ficere -fēcī -fectum	fail, give out; revolt from
deinde, dein	then, next
dēnique	finally
dēscendō -scendere -scendī -scēnsum	climb down, descend
dēserō -ere dēseruī dēsertum	leave, desert, abandon
dēsīderō -āre	long for, desire greatly
dēsinō -sinere -siī -situm	leave off, cease
dēsum -esse -fuī	be lacking
deus -ī m.; dea -ae f.	god; goddess
dexter -tra -trum	right; dextera -ae f.: right hand
dīcō dīcere dīxī dictum	say; causam dīcere, plead a case; diem dīcere, appoint a day
diēs diēī m./f.	day
differō differre distulī dīlātum	scatter; publish, divulge; differ; defer, postpone
difficilis -e	not easy, hard, difficult
dīgnitās -ātis f.	worth, reputation, honor
dīgnus -a -um	worthy
dīligō -ligere -lēxī -lēctum	choose, cherish, love
dīmittō -mittere -mīsī -missum	send away
discēdō -ere -cessī -cessum	go away, depart

disciplīna -ae f.	training, instruction; learning, discipline
discō -ere didicī	learn
diū	for a long time
dīversus -a -um	different, diverse
dīves dīvitis	rich (poet. dīs, dītis)
dīvidō -ere dīvīsī dīvīsum	divide, separate
dīvitiae -ārum f. pl.	riches, wealth
dīvus -a -um	divine, godlike
dō dare dedī datum	give
doceō -ēre -uī doctum	teach
doleō -ēre doluī	feel pain or grief, grieve
dolor -ōris m.	pain, grief
dolus -ī m.	artifice, device, trick
dominus -ī m.; domina -ae f.	household master, lord; mistress
domus -ūs f.	house, home
dōnec	until
dōnō -āre	present with a gift (+ acc. of person and abl. of thing)
dōnum -ī n.	gift, present
dormiō -īre	sleep
dubitō -āre	hesitate, doubt
dubius -a -um	doubtful, sine dubiō, without a doubt, certainly
dūcō dūcere dūxī ductum	lead; uxōrem dūcere, marry
dulcis -e	sweet

dum	while (+ indic.); until (+ subj.); provided that (+ subj.)
duo duae duo	two
dūrus -a -um	hard, tough, harsh
dux ducis m./f.	leader, general

E

ecce	behold!
ēdīcō -dīcere -dīxī -dictum	declare
ēdō ēdere ēdidī ēditum	put forth, state, explain
ēdūcō -dūcere -dūxī -ductum	lead forth
efficiō -ficere -fēcī -fectum	bring about, complete; render (+ ut + subj.)
effundō -fundere -fūdī -fūsum	pour out
ego meī mihi mē	I, me
ēgredior ēgredī ēgressus sum	stride out, depart, disembark from (+ abl.)
ēgregius -a -um	distinguished, uncommon
ēligō ēligere ēlēgī ēlēctum	pick out, select
enim	for, indeed
eō	(adv.) there, to that place
eō īre iī/īvī itum	go
epistula -ae f.	letter
eques -equitis m.	horseman, knight
equus -ī m.	horse

ergō	therefore
ēripiō -ripere -ripuī -reptum	snatch away, rescue, save
errō -āre	go astray, wander
error -ōris m.	wandering; error, mistake
et	and
etiam	also, even
ex, ē	out of, from (+ abl.)
excipiō -cipere -cēpī -ceptum	take out
exemplum -ī n.	example, sample, copy
exeō -īre -iī -itum	go forth
exerceō -ercēre -ercuī -ercitum	train, exercise, carry on
exercitus -ūs m.	army
exigō -igere -ēgī -āctum	drive out; collect
exīstimō -āre	think, believe
experior -perīrī -pertus sum	try thoroughly, test, experience
exsilium -ī n.	exile, banishment
exspectō -āre	watch, wait, expect
extrēmus -a -um	farthest, situated at the end or tip, extreme

F

fābula -ae f.	account, tale, story
faciēs -ēī f.	form, appearance
facilis -e	easy
facinus facinoris n.	deed, crime

faciō facere fēcī factum	do, make
factum -ī n.	deed, accomplishment
fallō fallere fefellī falsum	deceive
falsus -a -um	deceptive, false
fāma -ae f.	rumor, fame
famēs -is f.	hunger, famine
familia -ae f.	household, family
fateor fatērī fassus sum	admit, confess; profess, declare; assent, say yes
fātum -ī n.	fate; death
fax facis f.	torch
fēlīciter	luckily
fēlīx -īcis	lucky
fēmina -ae f.	woman
ferē	almost
ferō ferre tulī lātum	bear, carry, endure
ferrum -ī n.	iron, iron weapon or implement
ferus -a -um	wild, fierce; fera -ae f.: wild animal
fessus -a -um	weary, tired
fidēlis -e	faithful
fidēs -eī f.	trust, faith
fīlia -ae f.; fīlius -ī m.	daughter; son
fingō fingere fīnxī fīctum	shape; invent
fīnis -is m.	end, boundary
fīō fierī factus sum	become, happen, be done

flamma -ae f.	flame, fire
fleō flēre flēvī flētum	weep
flōs flōris m.	flower, bloom
fluctus -ūs m	flood, billow, surf
flūmen -inis n.	stream, river
fluō fluere fluxī fluxum	flow
foedus -a -um	foul
fōns fontis m.	spring, fountain
for fārī fātus sum	report, say
fore	= futūrum esse
forem, forēs, foret	= essem, essēs, esset
fōrma -ae f.	shape; beauty
fors fortis f.	chance
forsitan, fortasse	perhaps, perchance
fortē	by chance
fortis -e	brave
fortūna -ae f.	fortune
forum -ī n.	market-place, forum
frangō frangere frēgī frāctum	break, shatter
frāter frātris m.	brother
frequēns -ntis	in large numbers, often
frōns frontis f.	forehead, brow; front
frūctus -ūs m.	fruit, crops; enjoyment, delight
frūmentum -ī n.	grain

fruor fruī frūctus sum	enjoy the produce of, profit by, use (+ abl.)
frūstrā	in vain
fuga -ae f.	flight, route
fugiō fugere fūgī fugitum	flee, escape
fugō -āre	put to flight
fundō fundere fūdī fūsum	pour, scatter
fūnus fūneris n.	funeral; death; dead body
furor -ōris m.	rage, fury

G

gaudeō gaudēre gāvīsus sum	rejoice
gaudium -ī n.	delight, joy, pleasure
gēns gentis f.	family, clan
genus generis n.	origin, lineage, kind
gerō gerere gessī gestum	bear, manage; bellum gerere, wage war
gīgnō gīgnere genuī genitum	beget, bear, bring forth
gladius -ī m.	sword
glōria -ae f.	glory, fame
gradus -ūs m.	step, pace; grade, rank
grātia -ae f.	favor, influence, gratitude
grātus -a -um	pleasant; grateful
gravis -e	heavy, serious

H	
habeō habēre habuī habitum	have, hold
haud	not
hīc	here; hinc: from here
hic haec hoc	this, these
hiems hiemis f.	winter
hodiē	today
homō hominis m.	human being
honestus -a -um	honorable
honor -ōris m.	honor, glory; office, post
hōra -ae f.	hour
hortor hortārī hortātus sum	urge strongly, advise, exhort
hospes hospitis m.	guest, guest-friend; stranger; host
hostis -is m./f.	stranger, enemy
hūc	to this place
hūmānus -a -um	human
humus -ī f.	ground; humī: on the ground

I	
iaceō iacēre iacuī	lie
iaciō iacere iēcī iactum	throw, hurl
iam	now; already
ibi	there
īctus -ūs m.	blow, stroke

LATIN: Alphabetic Listing

īdem eadem idem	the same
ideō	for this reason
igitur	therefore
ignis -is m.	fire
ille illa illud	that
illīc	at that place, there; illinc: from that place
illūc	to that place
imāgō -inis f.	image, form, figure
imperātor -ōris m.	commander
imperium -ī n.	command, power
imperō -āre	command, control
impetus -ūs m.	attack
impleō -ēre -plēvī -plētum	fill in, fill up
impōnō -ere -posuī -positum	put in, put on, impose, levy upon
in	in, on (+ abl.); into, onto (+ acc)
incidō incidere incidī	fall upon, fall into; happen
incipiō -cipere -cēpī -ceptum	begin
inde	from there, from then
indicō -āre	point out, show, make known
īnferō īnferre intulī illātum	bring upon, against; bellum īnferre: make war on
īnferus -a -um	low; īnferior: lower; īnfimus or īmus: lowest
ingenium -ī n.	disposition, ability, talent
ingēns ingentis	huge, enormous

ingrātus -a -um	unpleasant, disagreeable
ingredior -gredī -gressus sum	step in, enter
inimīcus -a -um	unfriendly
initium -ī n.	beginning
iniūria -ae f.	injustice, wrong, affront
inquam, inquis, inquit, inquiunt	say (used with direct speech)
īnstituō -stituere -stituī -stitūtum	undertake; equip
īnsula -ae f.:	island
integer -gra -grum	untouched, fresh, complete, whole
intellegō -legere -lēxī -lēctum	understand
intendō -tendere -tendī -tentum	stretch out, strain
inter	between, among; during (+ acc.)
interficiō -ficere -fēcī -fectum	kill
interim	meanwhile
interrogō -āre	put a question to, ask (+ acc.)
intersum -esse -fuī	to be between; take part in, attend (+dat.); interest, it is in the interest of (+ gen.)
intrā	within (+ acc.)
intrō -āre	enter
inveniō -venīre -vēnī -ventum	find; discover
invidia -ae f.	envy, jealousy, hatred
ipse ipsa ipsum	him- her- itself
īra irae f.	wrath, anger
īrāscor īrāscī īrātus sum	grow angry; īrātus -a -um: angry

is ea id	he, she, it
iste ista istud	that, that of yours; adv. istīc or istūc: over there; istinc: from over there
ita	thus, so
itaque	and so, therefore
item	likewise
iter itineris n.	journey, route
iterum	again
iubeō iubēre iussī iussum	bid, order
iūdex iūdicis m.	judge, juror
iūdicium -ī n.	judgment, decision, trial
iūdicō -āre	judge, decide
iugum -ī n.	yoke; ridge, chain of hills
iungō iungere iūnxī iūnctum	join
iūrō -āre	take an oath, swear; iūs iūrandum, oath
iūs iūris n.	right, justice, law
iūstus -a -um	right, just, fair
iuvenis -is m.	youth
iuvō iuvāre iūvī iūtum	help, assist; please, delight

L

labor -ōris m.	toil, exertion
labōrō -āre	toil, work; be in trouble or distress

lacrima -ae f.	tear
laedō laedere laesī laesum	injure by striking, hurt
laetus -a -um	glad, joyful
lapis lapidis m.	stone
lateō latēre latuī	lie hidden, be hidden
lātus -a -um	broad, wide
latus -eris n.	side, flank
laudō -āre	praise
laus laudis f.	praise, glory
lēgātus -ī m.	lieutenant, envoy
legiō -ōnis f.	legion
legō legere lēgī lēctum	gather, choose, read
levis -e	light, trivial
lēx lēgis f.	law
līber lībera līberum	free; līberī (m. pl.): freeborn children
liber librī m.	book
lībertās -ātis f.	freedom
libet libēre libuit or libitum est	it is pleasing (+ dat. + infin.)
libīdō -inis f.	passion, lust
licet	even though
licet licēre licuit licitum est	it is permitted (+ dat. + infin.)
līmen līminis n.	threshold
lingua -ae f.	tongue; language
littera -ae f.	letter, (pl.) literature

lītus -oris n.	shore
locus -ī m.	place; loca (n. pl.) region
longē	far, far off
longus -a -um	long, far
loquor loquī locūtus sum	speak, talk
lūmen luminis n.	light
lūna -ae f.	moon
lūx lūcis f.	light of day

M

maestus -a -um	sad, sorrowful; depressing
magis	more
magister magistrī m.	master, chief
māgnitūdō -inis f.	greatness, size
māgnus -a -um	great
māior māius	greater, older
māiōrēs māiōrum m.	ancestors
male	(adv.) badly
mālō mālle māluī	prefer
malus -a -um	bad, evil
maneō manēre mānsī mānsum	remain
manus -ūs f.	hand; band of men
mare -is n.	sea
marītus -ī m.	husband

māter mātris f.	mother
māteria -ae f.	material, subject matter; timber, lumber
maximus -a -um	greatest; (adv.) māximē: most, especially, very much
medius -a -um	middle, central
melior melius	better
membrum -ī m.	limb, member of the body
meminī meminisse	remember, recollect
memoria -ae f.	recollection, memory
mēns mentis f.	mind
mēnsa -ae f.	table
mereō merēre meruī meritum	deserve, merit; serve as a soldier
metuō metuere metuī	to fear, to dread
metus -ūs m.	fear, dread
meus -a -um	my
mīles -itis m.	soldier
mīlle (pl.) mīlia	thousand
minus -ōris n.	a smaller number or amount, less; (adv.) minus: to a smaller extent, less
mīror mīrārī mīrātus sum	wonder at, marvel at (+ acc.)
misceō miscēre miscuī mixtum	mix
miser misera miserum	wretched, pitiable
mittō mittere mīsī missum	send, let go

modo	just, just now; modo ... modo: now ... now, at one moment ... at another, sometimes ... sometimes
modus -ī m.	measure, manner, kind
moenia -ium n. pl.	walls, fortifications
mollis -e	soft, yielding, gentle
moneō monēre monuī monitum	warn, advise
mōns montis m.	mountain
mora -ae f.	delay, hindrance
morbus -ī m.	sickness, disease
morior morī mortuus sum	die
moror morārī morātus sum	delay
mors mortis f.	death
mortālis -e	liable to death, mortal
mōs mōris m.	custom, habit; (pl.) character
moveō -ēre mōvī mōtum	move
mox	soon
mulier -eris f.	woman
multitūdō -inis f.	multitude, number
multus -a -um	much, many; multō, by far
mundus -a -um	clean, neat, elegant
mundus -ī m.	world, universe, heavens
mūnus mūneris n.	gift, offering; duty, obligation; (pl.) gladiatorial show
mūrus -ī m.	wall
mūtō -āre	change

N

nam or **namque**	for, indeed, really
narrō -āre	relate, recount
nāscor nāscī nātus sum	be born
nātūra -ae f.	nature
nātus -ī m.	son
nāvis -is f.	ship
nē	lest, that not
ne (enclitic)	interrogative particle attached to the emphatic word in a question
nec	and not, nor; nec ... nec, neither ... nor; → neque
necesse (indecl. adj.)	necessary
necessitās -tātis f.	necessity, need
nefās	impiety, wickedness
negō -āre	deny, refuse
negōtium -ī n.	business
nēmō	no one (gen. nūllīus, dat. nūllī, abl. nūllō or nūllā → nūllus -a -um)
nemus nemoris n.	grove, forest
neque	and not, nor; neque ... neque, neither ... nor; → nec
nesciō -scīre	not know, be ignorant
niger nigra nigrum	black
nihil, nīl	nothing; not at all
nimis or **nimium**	excessively

nimius -a -um	too much, excessive
nisi, nī	if not, unless
nōbilis -e	distinguished, noble; (as subst.) a nobleman or woman
noceō nocēre nocuī	harm
nōlō nōlle nōluī	be unwilling
nōmen -inis n.	name
nōn	not
nōndum	not yet
nōs nostrum/nostrī nōbīs nōs	we
nōscō nōscere nōvī nōtum	learn, (in perfect tenses) know
noster nostra nostrum	our
nōtus -a -um	well-known
novus -a -um	new
nox noctis f.	night
nūdus -a -um	naked, bare
nūllus -a -um	not any, no one
num	interrogative particle implying negative answer
nūmen -inis n.	divine will, deity
numerus -ī m.	number, amount
numquam	never
nunc	now
nūntius -ī m.	messenger; news

O

ob	against, on account of (+acc)
occīdō -cīdere -cīdī -cīsum	kill, cut down
occupō -āre	seize, occupy; anticipate, do a thing first (+ infin.)
occurrō -currere -cucurrī -cursum	run to meet; come into one's mind
oculus -ī m.	eye
ōdī ōdisse	hate
odium -ī n.	hatred
offerō offerre obtulī oblātum	present, offer, expose
officium -ī n.	service, duty
ōlim	formerly, at that time
omnis -e	all, every, as a whole
onus oneris n.	load, burden
opera -ae f.	labor, activity, work
oportet -ēre -uit	it is proper, right (+ acc. + infin.)
oppidum -ī n.	town
ops opis f.	assistance, resources
optimus -a -um	best, excellent; (adv.) optimē
optō -āre	choose, select
opus operis n.	work
ōrātiō -ōnis f.	speech, address
orbis -is m.	circle; orbis terrārum: world
ōrdō -īnis m.	order, rank
orior orīrī ortus sum	arise, begin

ōrō -āre	pray
ōs ōris n.	mouth, face
os ossis n.	bone
ostendō ostendere ostendī ostentum	show, hold out
ōtium -ī n.	leisure

P

paene	almost
pār paris	equal
parcō parcere pepercī parsum	spare, be sparing of (+ dat.)
parēns -ntis m./f.	parent
pāreō pārēre pāruī	obey
pariō parere peperī partum	bring forth, give birth to; accomplish
parō -āre	prepare, acquire; parātus -a -um, ready
pars partis f.	part
parum	too little
parvus -a -um	small
pateō patēre patuī	lie open, extend; be evident or obvious
pater patris m.	father, ancestor
patior patī passus sum	permit, endure
patria -ae f.	fatherland, country
paucī -ae -a	few

paulō, paulum	to only a small extent, slightly, a little
pauper -eris	poor, lowly
pāx pācis f.	peace
peccō -āre	commit a wrong, injure
pectus -oris n.	chest, breast
pecūnia -ae f.	money
pecus -oris n.	cattle, sheep
pellō pellere pepulī pulsum	strike, beat, push, drive
pendō pendere pependī pēnsum	weigh, hang, suspend; pay
per	through (+acc.)
perdō -dere -didī -ditum	destroy
pereō -īre -iī -itum	perish, be lost
pergō pergere perrēxī perrēctum	continue, proceed
perīculum -ī n.	danger
permittō -mittere -mīsī -missum	yield, allow, permit
perpetuus -a -um	unbroken, perpetual
pertineō -tinēre -tinuī	extend over, reach; refer to, pertain to, be the business of
perveniō -venīre -vēnī -ventum	arrive, reach
pēs pedis m.	foot
petō petere petīvī petītum	seek, aim at
pietās -tātis f.	sense of duty, devotion, esp. between parents and children
pius -a -um	dutiful, devoted, just, pious
placeō placēre placuī placitum	please

plēbs plēbis f.	the common people
plēnus -a -um	full
plērumque	generally
plērus- plēra- plērumque	the greater part, very many, most, the majority
plūrimus -a -um	the greatest number of, very many; plūrimī, most people
plūs plūris n.	a greater amount or number, more
poena -ae f.	penalty, punishment
poēta -ae m.	poet
pondus ponderis n.	weight
pōnō pōnere posuī positum	put, place; put aside
pontus -ī m.	the open sea, the deep
populus -ī m.	people
porta -ae f.	gate
portō -āre	carry a load
pōscō pōscere popōscī	demand, claim; inquire into
possum posse potuī	be able
post	after (adv. and prep. +acc.)
posteā	afterwards
posterus -a -um	next, later
postquam	after
potēns potentis	able, powerful
potestās -ātis f.	power
potis -e	powerful, able

praebeō -ēre -uī -itum	furnish, supply, render
praeceptum -ī n.	rule, precept; command
praecipiō -cipere -cēpī -ceptum	anticipate, advise, warn
praeda -ae f.	booty, prey
praemium -ī n.	bounty, reward
praesēns -ntis	present, in person, ready
praesidium -ī n.	garrison, protection
praestō -stāre -stitī -stitum	excel, exhibit
praeter	by, along, past; besides, except (+ acc.)
praetereā	besides, moreover
praetor -ōris m.	praetor, one of the chief Roman magistrates
precor -ārī	pray, invoke
premō premere pressī pressum	press, pursue, overwhelm
pretium -ī n.	price, worth, reward; pretium operae: a reward for trouble
prex precis f.	prayers, entreaties
prīmum	at first, firstly
prīmus -a -um	first
prīnceps -cipis	first, chief
prīncipium -ī n.	beginning
prior prius	earlier, preceding
prius or priusquam	before
prīvātus -a -um	personal, private

prō	for, on behalf of, in proportion to (+abl.)
probō -āre	approve, prove; convince one (dat.) of a thing (acc.)
prōcēdō -cēdere -cessī -cessum	go forth, advance
procul	at a distance
prōdō prōdere prōdidī prōditum	publish, hand down; give over, betray
proelium -ī n.	battle
proficīscor -ficīscī -fectus sum	set forth, go
prohibeō -ēre -uī -itum	restrain, keep away
prōmittō -mittere -mīsī -missum	send forth, offer
prope	near, next; (comp.) propior, (superl.) proximus; (adv.) prope, nearly, almost
properō -āre	hasten, speed
prōpōnō -pōnere -posuī -positum	put forth, propose, present
proprius -a -um	one's own, peculiar
propter	because of (+ acc.)
prōsum prodesse profuī	be of use, do good, help (+ dat.)
prōtinus	at once, forthwith
prōvincia -ae f.	province; official duty
pūblicus -a -um	public, belonging to the state
pudor pudōris m.	sense of shame, modesty, propriety
puella -ae f.	girl; girl-friend
puer puerī m.	boy; slave
pūgna -ae f.	fist-fight; battle

pūgnō -āre	fight
pulcher -chra -chrum	beautiful
putō -āre	think, suppose

Q

quā	where, how
quaerō -rere -sīvī -sītum	seek, inquire
quālis -e	of what kind? what?
quam	how?; (after comparative) than
quamquam	however, although
quamvīs	however you like; although
quandō	when?; since; sī quandō: if ever
quantum	(adv.) how much? how greatly? how much! how greatly! as much as
quantus -a -um	(interr.) how great? (rel.) of what size, amount, etc.
quārē	how? why?
quasi	as if
quattuor	four
que	and (enclitic)
quemadmodum	in what manner, how
queror querī questus sum	complain of, lament
quī quae quod	who, which, what
quia	because
quīcumque quaecumque quodcumque	who-, whatever

quīdam quaedam quoddam	a certain one, someone
quidem	certainly, at least
quiēscō quiēscere quiēvī quiētum	keep quiet; sleep
quīn	(adv.) indeed, in fact; (conjunction) so that ... not (+ subj.)
quīppe	(adv.) indeed, surely
quis quid	who? what? which?
quisquam quicquam/quidquam	any (single) person, anyone at all
quisque quaeque quidque	each one, everyone
quisquis quidquid	whoever, whichever
quō	for which reason; to or in what place; to what end, for what purpose?
quōmodo	in what way, how?
quondam	formerly, once
quoniam	since, seeing that
quoque	also, too
quotiēns	how many times?

R

rapiō rapere rapuī raptum	seize, tear away
rārus -a -um	wide apart, loose, thin; rare, seldom
ratiō -ōnis f.	method, plan, reason
recēdō -cēdere -cessī -cessum	step back, recoil, recede, withdraw
recēns -ntis	fresh, new

recipiō -cipere -cēpī -ceptum	take back, receive; sē recipere, betake oneself, go
rēctus -a -um	straight, direct
reddō -dere -didī -ditum	return, give back
redeō -īre -iī -itum	go back, return
referō referre rettulī relātum	bring back; report
regiō -ōnis f.	boundary, region
rēgius -a -um	kingly, royal
rēgnum -ī n.	kingship, kingdom
regō regere rēxī rēctum	guide, rule
relinquō -linquere -līquī -lictum	abandon
reliquus -a -um	remaining, rest
reor rērī rātus sum	think, imagine, suppose, deem
reperiō -perīre -pperī -pertum	find, find out
repetō -petere -petīvī -petītum	demand, exact; revisit; call to mind, recollect; repeat
rēs reī f.	thing (rēs pūblica, commonwealth; rēs familiāris, family property, estate; rēs mīlitāris, art of war; rēs novae, revolution)
respicio -ere -spēxī -spectum	look back, regard, consider
respondeō -spondēre -spondī -spōnsum	answer
retineō -tinēre -tinuī -tentum	hold back, keep
reus -ī m.	defendant
revertō -vertere -vertī	turn back
revocō -āre	call back, recall
rēx rēgis m.	king

rīdeō -ēre rīsī rīsum	laugh, laugh at
rīpa -ae f.	bank of a river
rogō -āre	ask
rumpō rumpere rūpī ruptum	break, rupture
rūrsus	back, again
rūs rūris n.	country

S

sacer sacra sacrum	holy, sacred
sacerdōs -dōtis m./f.	priest, priestess
saeculum -ī n.	generation, age, century
saepe	often
saevus -a -um	fierce, raging, wrathful
salūs -ūtis f.	health, safety
sānctus -a -um	sacred, inviolable
sanguis -inis m.	blood
sānus -a -um	sound, sane
sapiēns -ntis	wise man
sapientia -ae f.	wisdom
satis, sat	(adv.) enough, sufficiently
saxum -ī n.	rock, cliff, crag
scelus -eris n.	crime, sin
scientia -ae f.	knowledge
scīlicet	certainly, of course

sciō -īre -īvī/-iī -ītum	know
scrībō scrībere scrīpsī scrīptum	write
secundus -a -um	following; favorable
sēcūrus -a -um	free from care, tranquil; careless
sed	but
sedeō sedēre sēdī sessum	sit
sēdēs -is f.	seat, abode, habitation
semel	once
semper	always, ever
senātus -ūs m.	senate
senex -is m.	old man, elder; senior, older
sēnsus -ūs m.	feeling, emotion, sense
sententia -ae f.	opinion, judgment
sentiō sentīre sēnsī sēnsum	perceive, feel, hear, see
sepulcrum -ī n.	place of burial, tomb, grave
sequor sequī secūtus sum	follow
sermō -ōnis m.	conversation, discourse
serviō -īre	be a slave, serve (+ dat.)
servō -āre	save, watch over
servus -ī m.	slave
seu	whether; seu … seu: whether … or → sīve
sī	if
sīc	in this manner, thus; sīc … ut: in the same way as

sīcut	just as
sīdus -eris n.	star, constellation
sīgnum -ī n.	sign, standard, mark
silva -ae f.	forest, grove
similis -e	like, similar
simul	at the same time
sine	without (+ abl.)
singulī -ae -a	one each
sinō sinere sīvī situm	allow, let go
sinus -ūs m.	fold of a garment; lap, bay, gulf
sīve	whether; sīve ... sīve: whether ... or → seu
socius -a -um	friendly, allied; socius -ī m.: partner, comrade
sōl sōlis m.	sun
soleō -ēre -uī -itum	be accustomed
sōlum	only, merely
sōlus -a -um	only, alone
solvō solvere solvī solūtum	release, set sail
somnus -ī m.	sleep, slumber; (pl.) dreams
sonō sonāre sonuī sonitum	sound, resound
soror -ōris f.	sister
sors sortis f.	lot, fate, destiny; oracle
spargō spargere sparsī sparsum	scatter
spatium -ī n.	space

speciēs -ēī f.	aspect, appearance
spectō -āre	look at, consider
spērō -āre	to hope
spēs speī f.	hope
spīritus -ūs m.	breath, life, spirit
statim	immediately
statuō -ere -uī -ūtum	set up, determine
stella -ae f.	star
stō stāre stetī statum	stand
studeō -ēre -uī	be eager, be zealous, care for (+ dat.)
studium -ī n.	eagerness, zeal
sub	under, close to (+acc. or abl.)
subeō -īre -iī -itum	go under; endure
subitō	suddenly, unexpectedly
sui sibi sē/sēsē	him- her- itself, themselves
sum esse fuī	be, exist
summus -a -um	highest, farthest, last
sūmō sūmere sūmpsī sūmptum	take up
super	over (adv. and prep. +acc.)
superbus -a -um	overbearing, proud, haughty
superī -ōrum m. pl.	those above, i.e. the gods
superō -āre	overcome, surpass, defeat
supersum -esse -fuī	remain, survive; be superfluous (to)
superus -a -um	situated above, upper

supplicium -ī n.	punishment, penalty
suprā	above, beyond (adv. and prep. +acc.)
surgō surgere surrēxī surrēctum	rise
suscipiō -cipere -cēpī ceptum	take up
sustineō sustinēre sustinuī sustentum	hold up, sustain
suus -a -um	his own, her own, its own

T

taceō -ēre -uī -itum	be silent; tacitus -a -um, silent
tālis tāle	such
tam	so, so much
tamen	nevertheless, still
tamquam	so as, just as
tandem	finally
tangō tangere tetigī tāctum	touch
tantum, tantummodo	only
tantus -a -um	so great, so much
tardus -a -um	slow, sluggish, lingering
tēctum -ī n.	roof; building, house
tegō tegere tēxī tēctum	cover, conceal
tellus tellūris f.	earth
tēlum -ī n.	missile, weapon, spear
tempestas -tātis f.	period of time, season; bad weather, storm

templum -ī n.	consecrated ground; temple
temptō -āre	try, test
tempus -oris n.	time
tendō tendere tetendī tentum	stretch, extend, direct (one's steps or course)
tenebrae -brārum f. pl.	darkness, the shadows
teneō -ēre -uī tentum	hold, keep
tener -era -erum	tender
tergum -ī n.	back, rear; ā tergō: from the rear
terra -ae f.	land
terreō terrēre terruī territum	terrify, frighten
tertius -a -um	third
testis -is m.	witness
timeō -ēre -uī	to fear, to dread
timor -ōris m.	fear
tollō tollere sustulī sublātum	raise up, destroy
tot	so many
tōtus -a -um	whole, entire
trādō -dere -didī -ditum	hand over, yield
trahō trahere trāxī trāctum	drag, draw
trānseō -īre -iī -itum	go across
trēs tria	three
tribūnus -ī m.	tribune, title of various Roman officials, as mīlitum, plēbis, aerāriī
trīstis -e	sad, solemn, grim

tū tuī tibi tē	you (sing.)
tum or tunc	then
turba -ae f.	crowd, uproar
turbō -āre	disturb, confuse
turpis -e	ugly, unsightly; disgraceful
tūtus -a -um	safe, protected
tuus -a -um	your

U

ubi	where, when
ūllus -a -um	any, anyone
ultimus -a -um	farthest, final, last, ultimate
ultrā	beyond, further (adv. and prep. + acc.)
umbra -ae f.	shade, shadow
umquam	ever
unda -ae f.	wave, flowing water, water
unde	from where
undique	from all sides, on all sides
ūnus -a -um	one
urbs urbis f.	city
ūsque	up to; continuously
ūsus -ūs m.	use, experience
ut, utī	as (+ indic.); so that, with the result that (+ subj.)

uterque utraque utrumque	each of two
ūtilis -e	useful
ūtor ūtī ūsus sum	use, consume, employ (+ abl.)
utrum	whether; utrum ... an: whether ... or
uxor uxōris f.	wife

V

vacō vacāre	be empty, open, unoccupied
vacuus -a -um	empty
vagus -a -um	wandering, shifting
valeō valēre valuī	be strong, excel, be valid, prevail; valē: farewell!
validus -a -um	strong
vanus -a -um	empty; false, deceitful
varius -a -um	changing, varied, various
vātēs -is m.	poet, bard
ve	or (enclitic)
vehō vehere vēxī vectum	carry; vehor vehī vectus sum: travel, ride
vel	or else, or; even; vel ... vel: either ... or
velut	even as, just as
veniō venīre vēnī ventum	come
ventus -ī m.	wind
verbum -ī n.	word

vērē	truly
vereor verērī veritus sum	fear, stand in awe of
vērō	in fact, certainly, without doubt
vertō vertere vertī versum	turn
vērus -a -um	true
vester vestra vestrum	your
vestīgium -ī n.	footstep, footprint, track
vestis -is f.	garment, robe, clothing
vetō -āre vetuī vetītum	forbid
vetus veteris	old
via -ae f.	way, street
vīcīnus -a -um	neighboring, near
victor -ōris m.	conqueror
victōria -ae f.	victory
videō vidēre vīdī vīsum	see
vincō vincere vīcī victum	conquer
vinculum -ī n.	bond, fetter, tie
vīnum -ī n.	vine, wine
vir virī m.	man
virgō -inis f.	maiden, virgin, girl
virtūs -ūtis f.	valor, manliness, virtue
vīs f.	force; (acc.) vim, (abl.) vī; (pl.) vīrēs, strength
vīta -ae f.	life
vitium -ī n.	flaw, fault, crime

vītō -āre	avoid, shun
vīvō vīvere vīxī vīctum	live
vix	scarcely
vocō -āre	call
volō velle voluī	wish, be willing
volucer -cris -cre	flying
volucris -is f./m.	bird
voluntās -ātis f.	wish, desire
voluptās -ātis f.	pleasure, enjoyment
vōs	you (pl.); (gen.) vestrum/vestrī, (dat./abl.) vōbīs, (acc.) vōs
vōtum -ī n.	solemn promise, vow; hope
vōx vōcis f.	voice, utterance
vulgō	commonly
vulgus -ī n. and m.	the common people
vulnus -eris n.	wound
vultus -ūs m.	look, expression, face

1-100	
et	and
sum esse fuī	be, exist
quī quae quod	who, which, what
que	and (enclitic)
in	in, on (+ abl.); into, onto (+ acc)
nōn	not
hic haec hoc	this, these
ille illa illud	that
tū tuī tibi tē	you (sing.)
cum	with (prep. + abl.); when, since, although (conjunction + subj.)
ego meī mihi mē	I, me
quisquam quicquam/quidquam	any (single) person, anyone at all
is ea id	he, she, it
ad	to, up to, towards (+acc.)
ut, utī	as (+ indic.); so that, with the result that (+ subj.)
sī	if
sui sibi sē/sēsē	him- her- itself, themselves
omnis -e	all, every, as a whole
nec	and not, nor; nec ... nec, neither ... nor; → neque
sed	but
ā ab abs	from, by (+abl.)
ipse ipsa ipsum	him- her- itself

possum posse potuī	be able
aut	or
māgnus -a -um	great
ex, ē	out of, from (+ abl.)
suus -a -um	his own, her own, its own
dō dare dedī datum	give
maximus -a -um	greatest; (adv.) māximē: most, especially, very much
quam	how?; (after comparative) than
per	through (+acc.)
videō vidēre vīdī vīsum	see
faciō facere fēcī factum	do, make
dīcō dīcere dīxī dictum	say; causam dīcere, plead a case; diem dīcere, appoint a day
iam	now; already
atque	and in addition, and also, and; (after comparatives) than; simul atque, as soon as; → ac
ac	and in addition, and also, and; (after comparatives) than; simul ac, as soon as; → atque
alius -a -ud	other, another; ālias: at another time
rēs reī f.	thing (rēs pūblica, commonwealth; rēs familiāris, family property, estate; rēs mīlitāris, art of war; rēs novae, revolution)
habeō habēre habuī habitum	have, hold
animus -ī m.	spirit, mind

meus -a -um	my
deus -ī m.; dea -ae f.	god; goddess
multus -a -um	much, many; multō, by far
tuus -a -um	your
ferō ferre tulī lātum	bear, carry, endure
dē	down from, about, concerning (+ abl.)
nē	lest, that not
manus -ūs f.	hand; band of men
nūllus -a -um	not any, no one
nunc	now
nōs nostrum/nostrī nōbīs nōs	we
noster nostra nostrum	our
ūnus -a -um	one
diēs diēī m./f.	day
nihil, nīl	nothing; not at all
tum or tunc	then
enim	for, indeed
tamen	nevertheless, still
īdem eadem idem	the same
plūs plūris n.	a greater amount or number, more
rēx rēgis m.	king
nam or namque	for, indeed, really
locus -ī m.	place; loca (n. pl.) region
veniō venīre vēnī ventum	come

inter	between, among; during (+ acc.)
pars partis f.	part
volō velle voluī	wish, be willing
etiam	also, even
bonus -a -um	good
agō agere ēgī āctum	drive, do, act
terra -ae f.	land
pater patris m.	father, ancestor
neque	and not, nor; neque ... neque, neither ... nor; → nec
domus -ūs f.	house, home
at	but, but yet
corpus corporis n.	body
quoque	also, too
aliquis -quae -quod	some, any; si quis, si quid: anyone who, anything that
tōtus -a -um	whole, entire
plūrimus -a -um	the greatest number of, very many; plūrimī, most people
sīc	in this manner, thus; sīc ... ut: in the same way as
hīc	here; hinc: from here
iste ista istud	that, that of yours; adv. istīc or istūc: over there; istinc: from over there
urbs urbis f.	city
petō petere petīvī petītum	seek, aim at
iubeō iubēre iussī iussum	bid, order

vir virī m.	man
bellum -ī n.	war
vīta -ae f.	life
homō hominis m.	human being
tempus -oris n.	time
magis	more
prīmus -a -um	first
ubi	where, when
hostis -is m./f.	stranger, enemy
an	or (in questions); utrum ... an: whether ... or
mors mortis f.	death
tam	so, so much
eō īre iī/īvī itum	go
arma -ōrum n. pl.	arms, weapons
superus -a -um	situated above, upper
nisi, nī	if not, unless

101-200

vincō vincere vīcī victum	conquer
pōnō pōnere posuī positum	put, place; put aside
dum	while (+ indic.); until (+ subj.); provided that (+ subj.)
sine	without (+ abl.)
tantus -a -um	so great, so much

teneō -ēre -uī tentum	hold, keep
causa -ae f.	cause, reason; causā + preceding genitive, for the sake of
sequor sequī secūtus sum	follow
crēdō crēdere crēdidī crēditum	believe
accipiō -cipere -cēpī -ceptum	receive
virtūs -ūtis f.	valor, manliness, virtue
ante	before, in front of (adv. and prep. + acc.)
quaerō -rere -sīvī -sītum	seek, inquire
mittō mittere mīsī missum	send, let go
vīs f.	force; (acc.) vim, (abl.) vī; (pl.) vīrēs, strength
amor -ōris m.	love
caelum -ī n.	sky, heavens
sub	under, close to (+acc. or abl.)
nox noctis f.	night
ita	thus, so
rēgnum -ī n.	kingship, kingdom
populus -ī m.	people
autem	moreover, but, however
caput capitis n.	head
mare -is n.	sea
quīdam quaedam quoddam	a certain one, someone
māter mātris f.	mother
prō	for, on behalf of, in proportion to (+abl.)

quisquis quidquid	whoever, whichever
vōs	you (pl.); (gen.) vestrum/vestrī, (dat./ abl.) vōbīs, (acc.) vōs
capiō capere cēpī captum	seize
quia	because
dūcō dūcere dūxī ductum	lead; uxōrem dūcere, marry
ergō	therefore
nōmen -inis n.	name
quidem	certainly, at least
miser misera miserum	wretched, pitiable
fortūna -ae f.	fortune
novus -a -um	new
gravis -e	heavy, serious
vel	or else, or; even; vel ... vel: either ... or
longus -a -um	long, far
parvus -a -um	small
relinquō -linquere -līquī -lictum	abandon
saepe	often
fīō fierī factus sum	become, happen, be done
ōs ōris n.	mouth, face
alter altera alterum	other of two
semper	always, ever
deinde, dein	then, next
ignis -is m.	fire

modo	just, just now; modo ... modo: now ... now, at one moment ... at another, sometimes ... sometimes
timeō -ēre -uī	to fear, to dread
scelus -eris n.	crime, sin
dēbeō dēbēre dēbuī dēbitum	owe, be obliged
vīvō vīvere vīxī vīctum	live
fātum -ī n.	fate; death
vocō -āre	call
altus -a -um	high, lofty; deep
parō -āre	prepare, acquire; parātus -a -um, ready
mīles -itis m.	soldier
medius -a -um	middle, central
inquam, inquis, inquit, inquiunt:	say (used with direct speech)
post	after (adv. and prep. +acc.)
audiō -īre -īvī/-iī -ītum	hear, listen to
putō -āre	think, suppose
annus -ī m.	year
stō stāre stetī statum	stand
vōx vōcis f.	voice, utterance
genus generis n.	origin, lineage, kind
referō referre rettulī relātum	bring back; report
sciō -īre -īvī/-iī -ītum	know
mēns mentis f.	mind
reddō -dere -didī -ditum	return, give back

licet licēre licuit licitum est	it is permitted (+ dat. + infin.)
sōlus -a -um	only, alone
fugiō fugere fūgī fugitum	flee, escape
ūllus -a -um	any, anyone
nēmō	no one (gen. nūllīus, dat. nūllī, abl. nūllō or nūllā → nūllus -a -um)
nātūra -ae f.	nature
mōs mōris m.	custom, habit; (pl.) character
beneficium -ī n.	service, kindness
pectus -oris n.	chest, breast
fidēs -eī f.	trust, faith
patior patī passus sum	permit, endure
cūra -ae f.	care, concern
īra irae f.	wrath, anger
verbum -ī n.	word
prope	near, next; (comp.) propior, (superl.) proximus; (adv.) prope, nearly, almost
parēns -ntis m./f.	parent
puer puerī m.	boy; slave
moveō -ēre mōvī mōtum	move
dolor -ōris m.	pain, grief
gēns gentis f.	family, clan
modus -ī m.	measure, manner, kind
via -ae f.	way, street
quisque quaeque quidque	each one, everyone

amīcus -a -um	friendly; (as subst.) friend
pēs pedis m.	foot
imperium -ī n.	command, power

201-300

labor -ōris m.	toil, exertion
ingēns ingentis	huge, enormous
tālis tāle	such
parum	too little
apud	near, in the presence of (+acc.)
oculus -ī m.	eye
unda -ae f.	wave, flowing water, water
itaque	and so, therefore
vultus -ūs m.	look, expression, face
cadō cadere cecidī cāsum	fall, be killed
nātus -ī m.	son
quis quid	who? what? which?
trahō trahere trāxī trāctum	drag, draw
sanguis -inis m.	blood
metus -ūs m.	fear, dread
tantum, tantummodo	only
cōnsilium -ī n.	plan; council, group of advisors
melior melius	better
coniunx coniugis m./f.	spouse, husband, wife

amō -āre	to love; amāns -ntis m./f.: lover
levis -e	light, trivial
duo duae duo	two
ferus -a -um	wild, fierce; fera -ae f.: wild animal
poena -ae f.	penalty, punishment
castrum -ī n.	fortress, (regularly plural, castra camp)
frāter frātris m.	brother
haud	not
malus -a -um	bad, evil
iaceō iacēre iacuī	lie
līber lībera līberum	free; līberī (m. pl.): freeborn children
iter itineris n.	journey, route
ferrum -ī n.	iron, iron weapon or implement
spēs speī f.	hope
puella -ae f.	girl; girl-friend
silva -ae f.	forest, grove
bene	well
fīnis -is m.	end, boundary
optimus -a -um	best, excellent; (adv.) optimē
gerō gerere gessī gestum	bear, manage; bellum gerere, wage war
ne (enclitic)	interrogative particle attached to the emphatic word in a question
dux ducis m./f.	leader, general
premō premere pressī pressum	press, pursue, overwhelm
dominus -ī m.; domina -ae f.	household master, lord; mistress

mōns montis m.	mountain
summus -a -um	highest, farthest, last
uterque utraque utrumque	each of two
saevus -a -um	fierce, raging, wrathful
lītus -oris n.	shore
soleō -ēre -uī -itum	be accustomed
mīlle (pl.) mīlia	thousand
equus -ī m.	horse
dūrus -a -um	hard, tough, harsh
cōgō cōgere coēgī coāctum	drive together; compel
numquam	never
prīmum	at first, firstly
morior morī mortuus sum	die
carmen -inis n.	song
tēlum -ī n.	missile, weapon, spear
ratiō -ōnis f.	method, plan, reason
umbra -ae f.	shade, shadow
ars artis f.	skill
tot	so many
dexter -tra -trum	right; dextera -ae f.: right hand
sīgnum -ī n.	sign, standard, mark
laetus -a -um	glad, joyful
quālis -e	of what kind? what?
lēx lēgis f.	law

perīculum -ī n.	danger
nāscor nāscī nātus sum	be born
exercitus -ūs m.	army
pereō -īre -iī -itum	perish, be lost
minus -ōris n.	a smaller number or amount, less; (adv.) minus: to a smaller extent, less
ventus -ī m.	wind
audeō audēre ausus sum	dare, be eager
contrā	against, opposite (adv. and prep. +acc.)
aqua -ae f.	water
rapiō rapere rapuī raptum	seize, tear away
simul	at the same time
trīstis -e	sad, solemn, grim
mūnus mūneris n.	gift, offering; duty, obligation; (pl.) gladiatorial show
iuvenis -is m.	youth
fāma -ae f.	rumor, fame
adsum adesse adfuī	be present
vērō	in fact, certainly, without doubt
pār paris	equal
vester vestra vestrum	your
flūmen -inis n.	stream, river
quīcumque quaecumque quodcumque	who-, whatever
certus -a -um	sure, fixed
fortis -e	brave

placeō placēre placuī placitum	please
vertō vertere vertī versum	turn
servō -āre	save, watch over
honor -ōris m.	honor, glory; office, post
dīgnus -a -um	worthy
cūnctus -a -um	entire all together
tollō tollere sustulī sublātum	raise up, destroy
negō -āre	deny, refuse
vetus veteris	old
eques -equitis m.	horseman, knight
trādō -dere -didī -ditum	hand over, yield
flamma -ae f.	flame, fire
lūx lūcis f.	light of day
unde	from where

301-400

redeō -īre -iī -itum	go back, return
sentiō sentīre sēnsī sēnsum	perceive, feel, hear, see
aurum -ī n.	gold
cēdō cēdere cessī cessum	go, move; yield
quō	for which reason; to or in what place; to what end, for what purpose?
saxum -ī n.	rock, cliff, crag
ve	or (enclitic)
aetās -tātis f.	age, time of life

LATIN: Frequency Listing

fēlīx -īcis	lucky
loquor loquī locūtus sum	speak, talk
quantus -a -um	(interr.) how great? (rel.) of what size, amount, etc.
coepī coepisse coeptus	begin
igitur	therefore
iūs iūris n.	right, justice, law
mūtō -āre	change
inveniō -venīre -vēnī -ventum	find; discover
prīnceps -cipis	first, chief
ops opis f.	assistance, resources
recipiō -cipere -cēpī -ceptum	take back, receive; sē recipere, betake oneself, go
sōl sōlis m.	sun
cōnsul -ulis m.	consul
orbis -is m.	circle; orbis terrārum: world
turba -ae f.	crowd, uproar
ager agrī m.	field
solvō solvere solvī solūtum	release, set sail
vitium -ī n.	flaw, fault, crime
vulnus -eris n.	wound
inde	from there, from then
senātus -ūs m.	senate
ūtor ūtī ūsus sum	use, consume, employ (+ abl.)
cōpia -ae f.	abundance; (pl.) troops

opus operis n.	work
colō colere coluī cultum	inhabit, cultivate
vōtum -ī n.	solemn promise, vow; hope
iugum -ī n.	yoke; ridge, chain of hills
quā	where, how
tellus tellūris f.	earth
numerus -ī m.	number, amount
cōgnōscō -gnōscere -gnōvī -gnitum	learn, understand
victor -ōris m.	conqueror
satis, sat	(adv.) enough, sufficiently
patria -ae f.	fatherland, country
seu	whether; seu ... seu: whether ... or → sīve
cāsus -ūs m.	a fall; chance, accident
frangō frangere frēgī frāctum	break, shatter
cīvitās -ātis f.	citizenship, state
nōscō nōscere nōvī nōtum	learn, (in perfect tenses) know
proelium -ī n.	battle
ēripiō -ripere -ripuī -reptum	snatch away, rescue, save
mundus -ī m.	world, universe, heavens
cursus -ūs m.	course, advance
vix	scarcely
nāvis -is f.	ship
lacrima -ae f.	tear
hūmānus -a -um	human

mollis -e	soft, yielding, gentle
maneō manēre mānsī mānsum	remain
āgmen -minis n.	line of march
sīdus -eris n.	star, constellation
glōria -ae f.	glory, fame
diū:	for a long time
sīve	whether; sīve ... sīve: whether ... or → seu
tamquam	so as, just as
fuga -ae f.	flight, route
tūtus -a -um	safe, protected
auris -is f.	ear
aliēnus -a -um	foreign, strange
hūc	to this place
taceō -ēre -uī -itum	be silent; tacitus -a -um, silent
legiō -ōnis f.	legion
ostendō ostendere ostendī ostentum	show, hold out
socius -a -um	friendly, allied; socius -ī m.: partner, comrade
prōsum prodesse profuī	be of use, do good, help (+ dat.)
āra -ae f.	altar
lūmen luminis n.	light
tegō tegere tēxī tēctum	cover, conceal
turpis -e	ugly, unsightly; disgraceful
voluptās -ātis f.	pleasure, enjoyment

adhūc	thus far, to this point
grātia -ae f.	favor, influence, gratitude
iniūria -ae f.	injustice, wrong, affront
latus -eris n.	side, flank
dulcis -e	sweet
postquam	after
extrēmus -a -um	farthest, situated at the end or tip, extreme
tēctum -ī n.	roof; building, house
ingenium -ī n.	disposition, ability, talent
pāx pācis f.	peace
canō canere cecinī cantum	sing
iuvō iuvāre iūvī iūtum	help, assist; please, delight
campus -ī m.	plain, field
claudō claudere clausī clausum	close, shut
doceō -ēre -uī doctum	teach
excipiō -cipere -cēpī -ceptum	take out
clārus -a -um	clear, distinguished
illīc	at that place, there; illinc: from that place
procul	at a distance
sacer sacra sacrum	holy, sacred
mora -ae f.	delay, hindrance
longē	far, far off

401-500

super	over (adv. and prep. +acc.)
errō -āre	go astray, wander
sēdēs -is f.	seat, abode, habitation
cūr	why?
coma -ae f.	hair, tresses
aiō	say, affirm, say yes; ut āiunt: as they say
gaudeō gaudēre gāvīsus sum	rejoice
beātus -a -um	happy, blessed, prosperous, fortunate
perveniō -venīre -vēnī -ventum	arrive, reach
vērus -a -um	true
incipiō -cipere -cēpī -ceptum	begin
parcō parcere pepercī parsum	spare, be sparing of (+ dat.)
vestis -is f.	garment, robe, clothing
similis -e	like, similar
caedēs -is f.	killing, slaughter
ōrdō -īnis m.	order, rank
optō -āre	choose, select
virgō -inis f.	maiden, virgin, girl
legō legere lēgī lēctum	gather, choose, read
aura -ae f.	breeze
impetus -ūs m.	attack
fōrma -ae f.	shape; beauty
praestō -stāre -stitī -stitum	excel, exhibit

aequor aequoris n.	level surface, sea, plain
misceō miscēre miscuī mixtum	mix
spatium -ī n.	space
tandem	finally
īnferus -a -um	low; īnferior: lower; īnfimus or īmus: lowest
metuō metuere metuī	to fear, to dread
temptō -āre	try, test
trānseō -īre -iī -itum	go across
ultimus -a -um	farthest, final, last, ultimate
addō -dere -didī -ditum	give to
grātus -a -um	pleasant; grateful
laudō -āre	praise
nōndum	not yet
impōnō -ere -posuī -positum	put in, put on, impose, levy upon
somnus -ī m.	sleep, slumber; (pl.) dreams
aciēs -ēī f.	edge; line of battle
rūrsus	back, again
cupiō -ere -īvī -ītum	desire
exspectō -āre	watch, wait, expect
compōnō -pōnere posuī positum	build, construct, arrange
laus laudis f.	praise, glory
absum abesse āfuī	be away, absent
ūsus -ūs m.	use, experience
velut	even as, just as

comes comitis m./f.	companion, comrade; attendant, follower
ob	against, on account of (+acc).
studium -ī n.	eagerness, zeal
facilis -e	easy
nūmen -inis n.	divine will, deity
sapiēns -ntis	wise man
sūmō sūmere sūmpsī sūmptum	take up
nōbilis -e	distinguished, noble; (as subst.) a nobleman or woman
quīn	(adv.) indeed, in fact; (conjunction) so that ... not (+ subj.)
fleō flēre flēvī flētum	weep
nōlō nōlle nōluī	be unwilling
plēnus -a -um	full
adversus (-um)	(adv. and prep.) facing, opposite, against, opposed (to)
nemus nemoris n.	grove, forest
cārus -a -um	dear
dēsum -esse -fuī	be lacking
lēgātus -ī m.	lieutenant, envoy
discō -ere didicī	learn
furor -ōris m.	rage, fury
amnis -is m.	river, torrent
arbor arboris f.	tree
mox	soon

eō	(adv.) there, to that place
cīvis -is m./f.	citizen
occupō -āre	seize, occupy; anticipate, do a thing first (+ infin.)
spectō -āre	look at, consider
tergum -ī n.	back, rear; ā tergō: from the rear
crīmen -inis n.	verdict, accusation
dōnum -ī n.	gift, present
nōtus -a -um	well-known
sinus -ūs m.	fold of a garment; lap, bay, gulf
faciēs -ēī f.	form, appearance
rumpō rumpere rūpī ruptum	break, rupture
membrum -ī m.	limb, member of the body
umquam	ever
aspiciō -ere -spēxī -spectum	look to or at, behold
prius or priusquam	before
templum -ī n.	consecrated ground; temple
āmittō -mittere -mīsī -missum	let go, send away
pōscō pōscere popōscī	demand, claim; inquire into
perdō -dere -didī -ditum	destroy
quamvīs	however you like; although
tener -era -erum	tender
currus -ūs m.	chariot
precor -ārī	pray, invoke
anima -ae f.	breath, spirit

contingō -tingere -tigī -tactum	touch, be contiguous to
lībertās -ātis f.	freedom
servus -ī m.	slave
soror -ōris f.	sister
fluctus -ūs m	flood, billow, surf
quīppe	(adv.) indeed, surely
exigō -igere -ēgī -āctum	drive out; collect

501-600

fēmina -ae f.	woman
nimius -a -um	too much, excessive
fallō fallere fefellī falsum	deceive
mīror mīrārī mīrātus sum	wonder at, marvel at (+ acc.)
classis -is f.	class, division, fleet
sedeō sedēre sēdī sessum	sit
singulī -ae -a	one each
mūrus -ī m.	wall
noceō nocēre nocuī	harm
quoniam	since, seeing that
fax facis f.	torch
intellegō -legere -lēxī -lēctum:	understand
iungō iungere iūnxī iūnctum	join
afferō afferre attulī allātum	bring to
cōgitō -āre	think, reflect

līmen līminis n.	threshold
pūblicus -a -um	public, belonging to the state
queror querī questus sum	complain of, lament
exemplum -ī n.	example, sample, copy
prex precis f.	prayers, entreaties
dubitō -āre	hesitate, doubt
odium -ī n.	hatred
fundō fundere fūdī fūsum	pour, scatter
fūnus fūneris n.	funeral; death; dead body
nesciō -scīre	not know, be ignorant
prior prius	earlier, preceding
ūsque	up to; continuously
dubius -a -um	doubtful, sine dubiō, without a doubt, certainly
tendō tendere tetendī tentum	stretch, extend, direct (one's steps or course)
pecūnia -ae f.	money
quemadmodum	in what manner, how
spargō spargere sparsī sparsum	scatter
trēs tria	three
tangō tangere tetigī tāctum	touch
respondeō -spondēre -spondī -spōnsum	answer
timor -ōris m.	fear
properō -āre	hasten, speed
subeō -īre -iī -itum	go under; endure

valeō valēre valuī	be strong, excel, be valid, prevail; valē: farewell!
condō -dere -didī -ditum	build, found; store up; hide, conceal
nefās	impiety, wickedness
quondam	formerly, once
auxilium -ī n.	support, assistance; (pl.) auxiliary forces
dēserō -ere dēseruī dēsertum	leave, desert, abandon
nūdus -a -um	naked, bare
auctor -ōris m.	originator, founder
animal -ālis n.	a living being, an animal
decus decoris n.	beauty, grace; ornament, glory, honor
salūs -ūtis f.	health, safety
pateō patēre patuī	lie open, extend; be evident or obvious
rogō -āre	ask
uxor uxōris f.	wife
abeō -īre -iī -itum	go away
regō regere rēxī rēctum	guide, rule
adeō	(adv.) to such a degree, so
auferō auferre abstulī ablātum	take away
quantum	(adv.) how much? how greatly? how much! how greatly! as much as
senex -is m.	old man, elder; senior, older
frōns frontis f.	forehead, brow; front
propter	because of (+ acc.)
rēgius -a -um	kingly, royal

currō currere cucurrī cursum	run
pellō pellere pepulī pulsum	strike, beat, push, drive
dīves dīvitis	rich (poet. dīs, dītis)
iūdicō -āre	judge, decide
pecus -oris n.	cattle, sheep
potēns potentis	able, powerful
scrībō scrībere scrīpsī scrīptum	write
pulcher -chra -chrum	beautiful
surgō surgere surrēxī surrēctum	rise
cēterum	for the rest, in addition, however that may be
careō -ēre -uī	lack (+ abl.)
efficiō -ficere -fēcī -fectum	bring about, complete; render (+ ut + subj.)
ōlim	formerly, at that time
sermō -ōnis m.	conversation, discourse
exerceō -ercēre -ercuī -ercitum	train, exercise, carry on
gradus -ūs m.	step, pace; grade, rank
agitō -āre	drive
fortē	by chance
honestus -a -um	honorable
moror morārī morātus sum	delay
praesidium -ī n.	garrison, protection
sonō sonāre sonuī sonitum	sound, resound
praebeō -ēre -uī -itum	furnish, supply, render

regiō -ōnis f.	boundary, region
sententia -ae f.	opinion, judgment
ācer ācris ācre	sharp, piercing
suprā	above, beyond (adv. and prep. +acc.)
brevis -e	short, shallow, brief
citus -a -um	swift; citō swiftly
cornu -ūs n.	horn
ingrātus -a -um:	unpleasant, disagreeable
moenia -ium n. pl.	walls, fortifications
vinculum -ī n.	bond, fetter, tie
adeō -īre -iī -itum	go to
cēterus -a -um	the others, the rest
exeō -īre -iī -itum	go forth
mālō mālle māluī	prefer
speciēs -ēī f.	aspect, appearance
ultrā	beyond, further (adv. and prep. + acc.)

601-700

certē	certainly, surely
imperō -āre	command, control
male	(adv.) badly
prohibeō -ēre -uī -itum	restrain, keep away
clāmor -ōris m.	outcry, shout
dōnō -āre	present with a gift (+ acc. of person and abl. of thing)

officium -ī n.	service, duty
committō -mittere -mīsī -missum	join, entrust to (+ dat.); perform, do
crēscō crēscere crēvī crētum	grow, increase
aequus -a -um	equal
factum -ī n.	deed, accomplishment
caedō caedere cecīdī caesum	strike, kill, cut down
exīstimō -āre	think, believe
accēdō -cēdere -cessī -cessum	approach
contemnō -temnere -tempsī -temptum	despise, scorn, disdain
pudor pudōris m.	sense of shame, modesty, propriety
antīquus -a -um	ancient, old-time, former
ārdeō ārdēre ārsī ārsum	blaze, glow; be eager
ibi	there
prōvincia -ae f.	province; official duty
quandō	when?; since; sī quandō: if ever
custōs custōdis m.	guardian
supersum -esse -fuī	remain, survive; be superfluous (to)
dēsinō -sinere -siī -situm	leave off, cease
fessus -a -um	weary, tired
praeda -ae f.	booty, prey
memoria -ae f.	recollection, memory
dīvidō -ere dīvīsī dīvīsum	divide, separate
pretium -ī n.	price, worth, reward; pretium operae: a reward for trouble
pontus -ī m.	the open sea, the deep

varius -a -um	changing, varied, various
vehō vehere vēxī vectum	carry; vehor vehī vectus sum: travel, ride
falsus -a -um	deceptive, false
niger nigra nigrum	black
oppidum -ī n.	town
pondus ponderis n.	weight
arvum -ī n.	ploughed land, field
arx arcis f.	citadel, castle; summit
sors sortis f.	lot, fate, destiny; oracle
vīnum -ī n.	vine, wine
dīversus -a -um	different, diverse
orior orīrī ortus sum	arise, begin
ecce	behold!
quamquam	however, although
cōnferō cōnferre contulī collātum	collect, bring to
facinus facinoris n.	deed, crime
retineō -tinēre -tinuī -tentum	hold back, keep
spērō -āre	to hope
plēbs plēbis f.	the common people
pūgna -ae f.	fist-fight; battle
repetō -petere -petīvī -petītum	demand, exact; revisit; call to mind, recollect; repeat
cōnstituō -stituere -stituī -stitūtum	establish, put together
dēfendō -fendere -fendī -fēnsum	defend, ward off
marītus -ī m.	husband

cernō cernere crēvī crētum	discern, separate
superbus -a -um	overbearing, proud, haughty
adversus -a -um	facing, opposed; unfavorable
morbus -ī m.	sickness, disease
sānctus -a -um	sacred, inviolable
commūnis -e	common, general
dēdūcō -dūcere -dūxī -ductum	launch, lead away
rīpa -ae f.	bank of a river
concēdō -cēdere -cessī -cessum	yield, withdraw
hōra -ae f.	hour
vetō -āre vetuī vetītum	forbid
cohors cohortis f.	cohort, band, troop
gīgnō gīgnere genuī genitum	beget, bear, bring forth
superō -āre	overcome, surpass, defeat
maestus -a -um	sad, sorrowful; depressing
meminī meminisse	remember, recollect
impleō -ēre -plēvī -plētum	fill in, fill up
māgnitūdō -inis f.	greatness, size
vacuus -a -um	empty
vagus -a -um	wandering, shifting
vulgus -ī n. and m.	the common people
deficiō -ficere -fēcī -fectum	fail, give out; revolt from
occurrō -currere -cucurrī -cursum	run to meet; come into one's mind
statuō -ere -uī -ūtum	set up, determine

ideō	for this reason
praemium -ī n.	bounty, reward
praetereā	besides, moreover
tertius -a -um	third
supplicium -ī n.	punishment, penalty
vātēs -is m.	poet, bard
astrum -ī n.	star; constellation
undique	from all sides, on all sides
canis -is m./f.	dog
ēdō ēdere ēdidī ēditum	put forth, state, explain
fateor fatērī fassus sum	admit, confess; profess, declare; assent, say yes
amīcitia -ae f.	friendship
aureus -a -um	golden; splendid
candidus -a -um	white, fair
interim	meanwhile
frūstrā	in vain
lateō latēre latuī	lie hidden, be hidden
os ossis n.	bone
sēcūrus -a -um	free from care, tranquil; careless
conveniō -venīre -vēnī -ventum	assemble, meet; agree
interficiō -ficere -fēcī -fectum	kill
appellō -pellāre	call, address, name

701-800

dolus -ī m.	artifice, device, trick
permittō -mittere -mīsī -missum	yield, allow, permit
spīritus -ūs m.	breath, life, spirit
intrā	within (+ acc.)
terreō terrēre terruī territum	terrify, frighten
fōns fontis m.	spring, fountain
invidia -ae f.	envy, jealousy, hatred
pūgnō -āre	fight
augeō augēre auxī auctum	increase
littera -ae f.	letter, (pl.) literature
moneō monēre monuī monitum	warn, advise
dīvitiae -ārum f. pl.	riches, wealth
experior -perīrī -pertus sum	try thoroughly, test, experience
superī -ōrum m. pl.	those above, i.e. the gods
ōtium -ī n.	leisure
vestīgium -ī n.	footstep, footprint, track
sinō sinere sīvī situm	allow, let go
decet decēre decuīt	it is right, proper, fitting (+ acc. + infin.)
effundō -fundere -fūdī -fūsum	pour out
prōmittō -mittere -mīsī -missum	send forth, offer
fingō fingere fīnxī fīctum	shape; invent
respicio -ere -spēxī -spectum	look back, regard, consider
imperātor -ōris m.	commander

vacō vacāre	be empty, open, unoccupied
color -ōris m.	color
discēdō -ere -cessī -cessum	go away, depart
gaudium -ī n.	delight, joy, pleasure
caecus -a -um	blind, unseeing; dark, obscure
libet libēre libuit or libitum est	it is pleasing (+ dat. + infin.)
centum	one hundred
cōnstō -stāre -stitī	agree; constat, it is established that (+ acc. and infin.)
lingua -ae f.	tongue; language
multitūdō -inis f.	multitude, number
aeternus -a -um	everlasting, eternal
circā	around (adv. and prep. +acc.)
ōrātiō -ōnis f.	speech, address
potestās -ātis f.	power
tardus -a -um	slow, sluggish, lingering
for fārī fātus sum	report, say
humus -ī f.	ground; humī: on the ground
testis -is m.	witness
īnferō īnferre intulī illātum	bring upon, against; bellum īnferre: make war on
cūrō -āre	watch over, look after, care for (+ acc.)
aes aeris n.	copper, bronze
celer -is -e	swift
prōcēdō -cēdere -cessī -cessum	go forth, advance

mēnsa -ae f.	table
pius -a -um	dutiful, devoted, just, pious
iūdicium -ī n.	judgment, decision, trial
victōria -ae f.	victory
damnō -āre	condemn
rārus -a -um	wide apart, loose, thin; rare, seldom
tempestas -tātis f.	period of time, season; bad weather, storm
imāgō -inis f.	image, form, figure
ōrō -āre	pray
praeter	by, along, past; besides, except (+ acc.)
cōnsulō -sulere -suluī -sultum	consult, plan (+ acc.); consider the interests of (+dat)
iterum	again
porta -ae f.	gate
intersum -esse -fuī	to be between; take part in, attend (+dat); interest, it is in the interest of (+ gen.)
libīdō -inis f.	passion, lust
sustineō sustinēre sustinuī sustentum	hold up, sustain
aliquandō	at some time, at length
māiōrēs māiōrum m.	ancestors
reperiō -perīre -pperī -pertum	find, find out
intrō -āre	enter
pietās -tātis f.	sense of duty, devotion, esp. between parents and children
barbarus -ī m.	foreigner, barbarian

culpa -ae f.	guilt, fault, blame
iūstus -a -um	right, just, fair
dōnec	until
fluō fluere fluxī fluxum	flow
necesse (indecl. adj.)	necessary
reor rērī rātus sum	think, imagine, suppose, deem
tenebrae -brārum f. pl.	darkness, the shadows
saeculum -ī n.	generation, age, century
dīmittō -mittere -mīsī -missum	send away
licet	even though
cinis cineris m./f.	ashes, embers
cōnsistō -sistere -stitī	take position; consist in, be composed of
recēns -ntis	fresh, new
aliter	otherwise, differently
laedō laedere laesī laesum	injure by striking, hurt
probō -āre	approve, prove; convince one (dat.) of a thing (acc.)
doleō -ēre doluī	feel pain or grief, grieve
quārē	how? why?
antequam	before
reliquus -a -um	remaining, rest
semel	once
ōdī ōdisse	hate
sīcut	just as
peccō -āre	commit a wrong, injure

sēnsus -ūs m.	feeling, emotion, sense
exsilium -ī n.	exile, banishment
cor cordis n.	heart; cordī est, it is pleasing to (+ dat.)
dēnique	finally
sapientia -ae f.	wisdom
statim	immediately
accidō -cidere -cidī	fall; happen
dēcernō -cernere -crēvī -crētum	determine, decide

801-900

occīdō -cīdere -cīdī -cīsum	kill, cut down
dēscendō -scendere -scendī -scēnsum	climb down, descend
hiems hiemis f.	winter
contineō -tinēre -tinuī -tentum	contain, restrain
dēferō -ferre -tulī -lātum	carry away, report
oportet -ēre -uit	it is proper, right (+ acc. + infin.)
tribūnus -ī m.	tribune, title of various Roman officials, as mīlitum, plēbis, aerāriī
bōs bovis m.	ox; gen. pl. boum
īrāscor īrāscī īrātus sum	grow angry; īrātus -a -um: angry
aeger aegra aegrum	sick
forum -ī n.	market-place, forum
offerō offerre obtulī oblātum	present, offer, expose
revocō -āre	call back, recall
cingō cingere cīnxī cīnctum	encircle, surround, gird

integer -gra -grum	untouched, fresh, complete, whole
validus -a -um	strong
alō alere aluī alitum	nourish
flōs flōris m.	flower, bloom
īctus -ūs m.	blow, stroke
colligō -ere -lēgī -lēctum	gather together, collect
pergō pergere perrēxī perrēctum	continue, proceed
praesēns -ntis	present, in person, ready
rēctus -a -um	straight, direct
lātus -a -um	broad, wide
praeceptum -ī n.	rule, precept; command
recēdō -cēdere -cessī -cessum	step back, recoil, recede, withdraw
utrum	whether; utrum ... an: whether ... or
famēs -is f.	hunger, famine
pariō parere peperī partum	bring forth, give birth to; accomplish
appāreō -ēre -uī	appear, become visible
quōmodo	in what way, how?
error -ōris m.	wandering; error, mistake
forsitan, fortasse	perhaps, perchance
convertō -vertere -vertī -versum	turn about, turn, change
proficīscor -ficīscī -fectus sum	set forth, go
secundus -a -um	following; favorable
aperiō aperīre aperuī apertum	open
castus -a -um	pure, spotless, chaste

iūdex iūdicis m.	judge, juror
lapis lapidis m.	stone
nimis or nimium	excessively
onus oneris n.	load, burden
opera -ae f.	labor, activity, work
pauper -eris	poor, lowly
āēr āeris m.	air
negōtium -ī n.	business
pāreō pārēre pāruī	obey
subitō	suddenly, unexpectedly
argentum -ī n.	silver, money
ūtilis -e	useful
aethēr aetheris n.	pure upper air, ether, heaven, sky
mereō merēre meruī meritum	deserve, merit; serve as a soldier
portō -āre	carry a load
proprius -a -um	one's own, peculiar
avis -is f.	bird
vanus -a -um	empty; false, deceitful
māteria -ae f.	material, subject matter; timber, lumber
paucī -ae -a	few
voluntās -ātis f.	wish, desire
ēgregius -a -um	distinguished, uncommon
difficilis -e	not easy, hard, difficult
gladius -ī m.	sword

cibus -ī m.	food
certō -āre	decide by contest; fight, compete, vie
initium -ī n.:	beginning
pertineō -tinēre -tinuī	extend over, reach; refer to, pertain to, be the business of
quattuor	four
turbō -āre	disturb, confuse
cōnsūmō -sūmere -sūmpsī -sūmptum	to use up, consume
corrumpō -rumpere -rūpī -ruptum	break up, destroy, ruin
incidō incidere incidī	fall upon, fall into; happen
paulō, paulum	to only a small extent, slightly, a little
hospes hospitis m.	guest, guest-friend; stranger; host
rīdeō -ēre rīsī rīsum	laugh, laugh at
aevum -i n.	eternity; lifetime, age
audāx audācis	bold, daring; reckless
posterus -a -um	next, later
praetor -ōris m.	praetor, one of the chief Roman magistrates
rūs rūris n.	country
differō differre distulī dīlātum	scatter; publish, divulge; differ; defer, postpone
vītō -āre	avoid, shun
prīvātus -a -um	personal, private
serviō -īre	be a slave, serve (+ dat.)
vereor verērī veritus sum	fear, stand in awe of
ingredior -gredī -gressus sum	step in, enter

addūcō -ere -dūxī -ductum	lead to, induce
hortor hortārī hortātus sum	urge strongly, advise, exhort
reus -ī m.	defendant
scīlicet	certainly, of course
comparō -āre	get ready, provide; compare
perpetuus -a -um	unbroken, perpetual
dēsīderō -āre	long for, desire greatly
celebrō -āre	frequent, throng, crowd
cōnficiō -ficere -fēcī -fectum	complete, accomplish; destroy, kill, consume
intendō -tendere -tendī -tentum:	stretch out, strain
iūrō -āre	take an oath, swear; iūs iūrandum, oath
sōlum	only, merely
auctōritās -ātis f.	influence, clout, authority
iaciō iacere iēcī iactum	throw, hurl
labōrō -āre	toil, work; be in trouble or distress

901-997

liber librī m.	book
lūna -ae f.	moon
prōtinus	at once, forthwith
aequē	equally
māior māius	greater, older
cōnor cōnārī cōnātus sum	try, attempt
cupīdō -inis f.	desire, eagerness, craving

ferē	almost
īnsula -ae f.	island
fīlia -ae f.; fīlius -ī m.	daughter; son
narrō -āre	relate, recount
necessitās -tātis f.	necessity, need
ēgredior ēgredī ēgressus sum	stride out, depart, disembark from (+ abl.)
poēta -ae m.	poet
decem	ten
amplus -a -um	large, spacious
aptus -a -um	fit, suitable
cōnsequor -sequī -secūtus sum	follow up, overtake, attain
frequēns -ntis	in large numbers, often
nūntius -ī m.	messenger; news
condīciō -ōnis f.	agreement, condition
convīvium -iī n.	banquet, feast
foedus -a -um	foul
fruor fruī frūctus sum	enjoy the produce of, profit by, use (+ abl.)
num	interrogative particle implying negative answer
albus -a -um	white
damnum -ī n.	damage, injury
frūctus -ūs m.	fruit, crops; enjoyment, delight
cēnseō cēnsēre cēnsuī cēnsum	assess, rate; think, decide
prōdō prōdere prōdidī prōditum	publish, hand down; give over, betray

LATIN: Frequency Listing

prōpōnō -pōnere -posuī -positum	put forth, propose, present
īnstituō -stituere -stituī -stitūtum	undertake; equip
item	likewise
magister magistrī m.	master, chief
stella -ae f.	star
ēdūcō -dūcere -dūxī -ductum	lead forth
frūmentum -ī n.	grain
suscipiō -cipere -cēpī ceptum	take up
quasi	as if
sacerdōs -dōtis m./f.	priest, priestess
vīcīnus -a -um	neighboring, near
caveō cavēre cāvī cautum	be on guard, beware
ēligō ēligere ēlēgī ēlēctum	pick out, select
familia -ae f.	household, family
paene	almost
praecipiō -cipere -cēpī -ceptum	anticipate, advise, warn
sānus -a -um	sound, sane
potis -e	powerful, able
prīncipium -ī n.	beginning
sepulcrum -ī n.	place of burial, tomb, grave
mortālis -e	liable to death, mortal
epistula -ae f.	letter
inimīcus -a -um	unfriendly
interrogō -āre	put a question to, ask (+ acc.)

cōnsuētūdo -inis f.	custom, habit
illūc	to that place
dīgnitās -ātis f.	worth, reputation, honor
fugō -āre	put to flight
afficiō -ficere -fēcī -fectum	affect, visit with (+ abl.)
adhibeō -hibēre -hibuī -hibitum	apply
caelestis -e	from or of heaven; caelestēs, the gods
mulier -eris f.	woman
dīvus -a -um	divine, godlike
arbitror arbitrārī arbitrātus sum	consider, think
posteā	afterwards
aedēs -is f.	building; (pl.) house
fābula -ae f.	account, tale, story
celeriter	quickly
plērus- plēra- plērumque	the greater part, very many, most, the majority
quiēscō quiēscere quiēvī quiētum	keep quiet; sleep
quotiēns	how many times?
scientia -ae f.	knowledge
cōnfiteor cōnfitērī cōnfessus sum	admit (a fact), confess (a crime); reveal, disclose
dīligō -ligere -lēxī -lēctum	choose, cherish, love
plērumque	generally
dormiō -īre	sleep
volucris -is f./m.	bird

LATIN: Frequency Listing

volucer -cris -cre	flying
creō -āre	produce, create; elect, choose
fidēlis -e	faithful
indicō -āre	point out, show, make known
hodiē	today
disciplīna -ae f.	training, instruction; learning, discipline
vērē	truly
aegrē	with difficulty
fore	= futūrum esse
forem, forēs, foret	= essem, essēs, esset
advertō -vertere -vertī -versum	turn towards
adveniō -īre -vēnī -ventum	come to, arrive at
pendō pendere pependī pēnsum	weigh, hang, suspend; pay
studeō -ēre -uī	be eager, be zealous, care for (+ dat.)
ascendō -ere -scendī -scēnsum	climb up, ascend
vulgō	commonly
breviter	briefly
fors fortis f.	chance
fēlīciter	luckily
revertō -vertere -vertī	turn back
ēdīcō -dīcere -dīxī -dictum	declare
mundus -a -um	clean, neat, elegant

GREEK

A

ἀγαθός –ή –όν	good, virtuous, brave, noble
ἀγγέλλω, ἀγγελῶ, ἤγγειλα, ἤγγελκα, ἤγγελμαι, ἠγγέλθην	report, tell
ἄγω, ἄξω, ἤγαγον, ἦχα, ἦγμαι, ἤχθην	lead, carry, bring; pass (time)
ἀγών ἀγῶνος, ὁ	contest; struggle
ἀδελφός –οῦ, ὁ	brother
ἀδικέω, ἀδικήσω, ἠδίκησα, ἠδίκηκα, ἠδίκημαι, ἠδικήθην	do wrong; injure
ἄδικος ἄδικον	unjust
ἀδύνατος –ον	impossible; powerless
ἀεί always	
αἷμα αἵματος, τό	blood
αἱρέω, αἱρήσω, 2 aor. εἷλον, ᾕρηκα, ᾕρημαι, ᾑρέθην	take, grasp, take by force; (mid.) choose
αἴρω, ἀρῶ, ἦρα, ἦρκα, ἦρμαι, ἤρθην	take up, lift up; remove
αἰσθάνομαι, αἰσθήσομαι, 2 aor. ᾐσθόμην, ᾔσθημαι	perceive, understand, hear, learn
αἰσχρός –ά –όν	ugly, shameful, disgraceful
αἰτέω, αἰτήσω, ᾔτησα, ᾔτηκα, ᾔτημαι, ᾐτήθην	ask (for), beg
αἰτία αἰτίας, ἡ	cause, origin; charge, accusation
αἴτιος αἰτία αἴτιον	responsible, guilty

ἀκούω, ἀκούσομαι, ἤκουσα, ἀκήκοα, plup. ἠκηκόη or ἀκηκόη, ἠκούσθην

listen (to), hear (of)

ἀκριβής –ές

exact, accurate, precise

ἀλήθεια ἀληθείας, ἡ

truth

ἀληθής –ές

true

ἀλίσκομαι, ἀλώσομαι, 2 aor. ἑάλων, ἑάλωκα

to be taken, conquered (act. supplied by αἱρέω)

ἀλλά

but

ἀλλήλων –οις

(oblique cases plural only) one another, each other

ἄλλος ἄλλη ἄλλο

other, another

ἄλλως

otherwise

ἅμα

at the same time; (prep.) together with (+dat.)

ἁμαρτάνω, ἁμαρτήσομαι, ἡμάρτησα, 2 aor. ἥμαρτον, ἡμάρτηκα, ἡμάρτημαι, ἡμαρτήθην

miss the mark (+gen.); fail, be wrong, make a mistake

ἀμείνων ἄμεινον

better, abler, stronger, braver (comp. of ἀγαθός)

ἀμφί

about, around

ἀμφότερος ἀμφοτέρα ἀμφότερον

both

ἄν

[marks verbs as potential (with optative), or generalizing (with subjunctive)]

ἀνά	up, on; throughout
ἀνάγκη ἀνάγκης, ἡ	necessity
ἀναιρέω, ἀναιρήσω, ἀνεῖλον, ἀνήρηκα, ἀνήρημαι, ἀνηρέθην	raise, take up; kill, destroy
ἄνευ	without (+gen.)
ἀνήρ ἀνδρός, ὁ	man, husband
ἄνθρωπος –ου, ὁ/ἡ	human being
ἀντί	opposite (+gen.)
ἄνω	up, upwards
ἄξιος ἀξία ἄξιον	worthy, deserving
ἀξιόω, ἀξιώσω, ἠξίωσα, ἠξίωκα, ἠξίωμαι, ἠξιώθην	consider worthy
ἀπαλλάσσω, ἀπαλλάξω, ἀπήλλαξα, ἀπήλλαχα, ἀπήλλαγμαι, ἀπηλλάχθην or ἀπηλλάγην	set free, release, deliver
ἅπας ἅπασα ἅπαν	all together
ἁπλῶς	simply, plainly
ἀπό	from (+gen.)
ἀποδίδωμι, ἀποδώσω, ἀπέδωκα, ἀποδέδωκα, ἀποδέδομαι, ἀπεδόθην	give back; render; allow; (mid.) sell
ἀποθνήσκω, ἀποθανοῦμαι, 2 aor. ἀπέθανον, ἀποτέθνηκα	die

ἀποκρίνω, ἀποκρινῶ, ἀπεκρινάμην, ἀπεκρίθη	separate, set apart; (mid.) answer, reply
ἀποκτείνω, ἀποκτενῶ, ἀπέκτεινα, ἀπέκτονα	kill
ἀπόλλυμι, ἀπολῶ, ἀπώλεσα, 2 aor. mid. ἀπωλόμην, pf. ἀπολώλεκα ("I have utterly destroyed") or ἀπόλωλα ("I am undone")	kill, destroy; (mid.) perish, die
ἄρα	therefore, then (drawing an inference)
ἄρα	[introduces a question]
ἀργύριον ἀργυρίου, τό	money
ἀρετή ἀρετῆς, ἡ	goodness, excellence; virtue; valor, bravery
ἀριθμός –οῦ, ὁ	number
ἄριστος ἀρίστη ἄριστον	best, noblest (superl. of ἀγαθός)
ἀρχή ἀρχῆς, ἡ	beginning, origin; rule, empire, realm; magistracy
ἄρχω, ἄρξω, ἦρξα, ἦργμαι, ἤρχθην	begin (+gen.); lead, rule, govern (+gen.)
αὖ, αὖθις	in turn, then, furthermore, again
αὐτίκα	at once, immediately
αὐτός αὐτή αὐτό	him- her- itself etc. (for emphasis); the same (with article); (pron.) him, her, it etc. (in oblique cases)

ἀφαιρέω, ἀφαιρήσω, ἀφεῖλον, ἀφήρηκα, ἀφήρημαι, ἀφηρέθην	take from, take away
ἀφίημι, ἀφήσω, ἀφῆκα, ἀφεῖκα, ἀφεῖμαι, ἀφείθην	send away, let go; let alone, neglect
ἀφικνέομαι, ἀφίξομαι, 2 aor. ἀφικόμην, ἀφῖγμαι	come to, arrive at

B

βαίνω, βήσομαι, 2 aor. ἔβην, βέβηκα	walk, come, go
βάλλω, βαλῶ, 2 aor. ἔβαλον, βέβληκα, βέβλημαι, ἐβλήθην	throw, hurl; throw at, hit (acc.) with (dat.)
βάρβαρος –ον	non-Greek, foreign; barbarous
βαρύς βαρεῖα βαρύ	heavy, grievous, tiresome
βασιλεύς βασιλέως, ὁ	king
βελτίων βέλτιον	better (comp. of ἀγαθός)
βίος βίου, ὁ	life
βλέπω, βλέψομαι, ἔβλεψα	see, look (at)
βοηθέω, βοηθήσω, ἐβοήθησα, βεβοήθηκα	help, assist (+dat.)
βουλεύω βουλεύσω, ἐβούλευσα, βεβούλευκα, βεβούλευμαι, ἐβουλεύθην	plan (to), decide (to); (mid.) deliberate
βουλή βουλῆς, ἡ	will, determination; counsel, piece of advice; council of elders

βούλομαι, βουλήσομαι,
βεβούλημαι, ἐβουλήθην

(+infin.) will, wish (to); be willing (to); ὁ βουλόμενος anyone who likes

βοῦς βοός, ὁ/ἡ

bull, ox, cow

βραχύς βραχεῖα βραχύ

brief, short

Γ

γάρ

for (explanatory), indeed, in fact (confirming)

γε

(enclitic) indeed; at least, at any rate

γένος γένους, τό

race, family; kind, class

γῆ γῆς, ἡ

earth

γίγνομαι, γενήσομαι, 2 aor.
ἐγενόμην, γέγονα, γεγένημαι,
ἐγενήθην

become; be born; happen, be

γιγνώσκω, γνώσομαι, ἔγνων,
ἔγνωκα, ἔγνωσμαι, ἐγνώσθην

come to know, learn; judge, think, or determine that (+acc. and infin.)

γλῶσσα γλώσσης, ἡ

tongue; language

γνώμη γνώμης, ἡ

thought, intelligence, opinion, purpose

γράμμα γράμματος, τό

letter, written character; (pl.) piece of writing, document(s)

γραφή γραφῆς, ἡ

a drawing, painting, writing; indictment

γράφω, γράψω, ἔγραψα, γέγραφα, γέγραμμαι, ἐγράφην	write
γυνή γυναικός, ἡ	woman, wife

Δ

δαίμων δαίμονος, ὁ/ἡ	spirit, god, demon
δέ	and; but
δέδοικα, δείσομαι, ἔδεισα	fear
δεῖ, δεήσει, impf. ἔδει	it is necessary, one must, one ought (+acc. and infin.)
δείκνυμι, δείξω, ἔδειξα, δέδειχα, δέδειγμαι, ἐδείχθην	show, point out
δεινός –ή –όν	awesome, terrible; clever, clever at (+infin.)
δέκα	ten
δέκατος –η –ον	tenth
δεσπότης –ου, ὁ	master (of the household); absolute ruler
δεύτερος –α –ον	second
δέχομαι, δέξομαι, ἐδεξάμην, δέδεγμαι, -εδέχθην	take, accept; welcome, entertain
δέω, δεήσω, ἐδέησα, δεδέηκα, δεδέημαι, ἐδεήθην	lack, miss, stand in need of (+gen.)

δή

surely, really, now, in fact, indeed (gives greater exactness)

δῆλος δήλη δῆλον

visible, clear, manifest

δηλόω, δηλώσω, ἐδήλωσα, δεδήλωκα, ἐδηλώθην

show, declare, explain

δῆμος δήμου, ὁ

the (common) people; country district (opp. πόλις)

διά

through, during, because of (+gen., acc.)

διαφέρω, διοίσω, 1 aor. διήνεγκα, 2 aor. διήνεγκον, διενήνοχα, διενήνεγμαι

carry in different ways, spread; differ; (impers.) διαφέρει it makes a difference to (+dat.)

διαφθείρω, διαφθερῶ, διέφθειρα, διέφθαρκα, διέφθαρμαι, διεφθάρην

destroy; corrupt

διαφορά –ᾶς, ἡ

difference, disagreement

διδάσκω, διδάξω, ἐδίδαξα, δεδίδαχα, δεδίδαγμαι, ἐδιδάχθην

teach

δίδωμι, δώσω, ἔδωκα, δέδωκα, δέδομαι, ἐδόθην

give, grant, offer

δίκαιος δικαία δίκαιον

right, just

δίκη δίκης, ἡ

justice, lawsuit, trial, penalty

διώκω, διώξομαι, ἐδίωξα, δεδίωχα, ἐδιώχθην

pursue

δοκέω, δόξω, ἔδοξα — think, suppose, imagine (+acc. and infin.); seem, seem good; (impers.)

δοκεῖ μοι — it seems to me

δόξα δόξης, ἡ — opinion, judgment; reputation, honor, glory

δοῦλος δούλου, ὁ — slave

δράω, δράσω, ἔδρασα, δέδρακα, δέδραμαι, ἐδράσθην — do, accomplish

δύναμαι, δυνήσομαι, ἐδυνήθην, δεδύνημαι — (+infin.) to be able (to), be strong enough (to)

δύναμις δυνάμεως, ἡ — power, strength, ability

δυνατός –ή –όν — strong, powerful, able

δύο — two

E

ἐάν (εἰ-ἄν) — if (+subj.)

ἑαυτοῦ ἑαυτῆς ἑαυτοῦ — him- her- itself (reflexive pron.)

ἐάω, ἐάσω, εἴασα — allow, permit (+acc. and infin.); let be, let alone

ἕβδομος –η –ον — seventh

ἐγώ ἐμοῦ, (pl.) ἡμεῖς, ἡμῶν — I, we

ἐθέλω, ἐθελήσω, ἠθέλησα, ἠθέληκα — (+infin.) wish (to); be willing (to)

ἔθνος ἔθνους, τό — nation

GREEK: Alphabetic Listing

εἰ — if (+indic. or opt.); εἴπερ if indeed

εἶδον, 2 aor. of ὁράω,
  act. infin. ἰδεῖν, mid.infin. ἰδέσθαι — I saw

εἶδος εἴδους, τό — form, shape, figure; class, kind, sort

εἰκός εἰκότος, τό — likelihood, probability; εἰκός (ἐστι) it is likely (+infin.) → ἔοικα

εἴκοσι(ν) — twenty

εἰκοστός –ή –όν — twentieth

εἶμι, infin. ἰέναι, ptc. ἰών, ἰοῦσα, ἰόν — I will go (fut. of ἔρχομαι)

εἰμί, ἔσομαι, impf. ἦν, infin. εἶναι — be, exist

εἶπον — I said, I spoke, 2 aor. → λέγω, φημί

εἰρήνη εἰρήνης, ἡ — peace

εἰς — into, to, towards (+acc.)

εἷς μία ἕν — one

εἶτα — then, next

εἴτε...εἴτε — whether...or

ἐκ, ἐξ — from, out of (+gen.)

ἕκαστος ἑκάστη ἕκαστον — each (of several)

ἑκάτερος ἑκατέρα ἑκάτερον — each (of two)

ἑκατόν — hundred

ἑκατοστός –ή –όν — hundredth

GREEK: Alphabetic Listing

ἐκεῖ	there
ἐκεῖνος ἐκείνη ἐκεῖνον	that person or thing; ἐκεῖνος... οὗτος the former...the latter
ἕκτος –η –ον	sixth
ἐλάσσων ἔλασσον	smaller, less, fewer (comp. of μικρός)
ἐλαύνω, ἐλῶ, ἤλασα, -ελήλακα, ἐλήλαμαι, ἠλάθην	drive, set in motion
ἐλεύθερος ἐλευθέρα ἐλεύθερον	free, independent
ἐλπίς ἐλπίδος, ἡ	hope; expectation
ἐμός ἐμή ἐμόν	my, mine
ἐν	in, among (+dat.)
ἐναντίος ἐναντία ἐναντίον	opposite, facing; opposing
ἔνατος –α –ον	ninth
ἕνεκα	on account of, for the sake of (+gen.)
ἔνθα	there
ἐννέα	nine
ἐνταῦθα	here, there
ἕξ	six
ἔξω	outside; except
ἔοικα, ptc. εἰκώς	be like, look like (+dat.); seem; befit

ἐπεί	after, since, when
ἔπειτα	then, next
ἐπί	at (+gen.); on (+dat.); on to, against (+acc.)
ἐπιστήμη –ης, ἡ	knowledge, understanding, skill
ἕπομαι ἕψομαι, 2 aor. ἑσπόμην	follow
ἔπος ἔπους, τό	word, speech, tale; prophecy
ἑπτά	seven
ἐργάζομαι, ἐργάσομαι, εἰργασάμην, εἴργασμαι	work, labor
ἔργον ἔργου, τό	work, achievement, exploit
ἔρομαι, ἐρήσομαι, 2 aor. ἠρόμην	ask, ask one about (+double acc.)
ἔρχομαι, fut. εἶμι or ἐλεύσομαι, 2 aor. ἦλθον, ἐλήλυθα	come, go
ἐρωτάω, ἐρήσομαι, 2 aor. ἠρόμην	ask someone (acc.) something (acc.); question, beg
ἕτερος ἑτέρα ἕτερον	the other (of two); other, another
ἔτι	still, yet
ἔτος ἔτους, τό	year
εὖ	well (opp. κακῶς); thoroughly, competently; happily, fortunately
εὐθύς εὐθεῖα εὐθύ immediately	straight, direct; (adv.)

εὑρίσκω, εὑρήσω, 2 aor. ηὗρον
or εὗρον, ηὕρηκα or εὕρηκα,
εὕρημαι, εὑρέθην

find (out), discover, devise

ἐχθρός –ά –όν

hated, hateful; hostile to (+dat.)

ἔχω, ἕξω or σχήσω, 2 aor. ἔσχον,
ἔσχηκα, impf. εἶχον

have, hold, keep

ἕως

until; while, so long as

Z

ζάω, ζήσω, ἔζησα, ἔζηκα

live

ζητέω, ζητήσω, ἐζήτησα, ἐζήτηκα

seek

ζῷον ζῴου, τό

living being, animal

H

ἤ

or; than (after a comparative);
ἤ...ἤ either...or

ἦ

truly (emphasizes what follows)

ἡγεμών ἡγεμόνος, ὁ

guide, leader, commander

ἡγέομαι, ἡγήσομαι, ἡγησάμην,
ἥγημαι

lead, be the leader; regard,
believe, think

ἤδη

already, now (of the immediate
past); presently (of the
immediate future)

ἡδονή –ῆς, ἡ	pleasure, enjoyment
ἡδύς ἡδεῖα ἡδύ	sweet, pleasant
ἥκω, ἥξω, pf. ἧκα	I have come, I am present
ἥλιος ἡλίου, ὁ	sun
ἡμέρα ἡμέρας, ἡ	day
ἡμέτερος ἡμετέρα ἡμέτρον	our
ἥσσων ἧσσον	less, weaker (comp. of κακός or μικρός)

Θ

θάλασσα θαλάσσης, ἡ	the sea
θάνατος θανάτου, ὁ	death
θαυμάζω, θαυμάσομαι, ἐθαύμασα, τεθαύμακα, τεθαύμασμαι, ἐθαυμάσθην	to be in awe (of), be astonished (at)
θεῖος θεία θεῖον	divine
θεός θεοῦ, ὁ/ἡ	god, goddess
θνήσκω, 2 aor. -έθανον, τέθνηκα, θανοῦμαι	to die, be dying
θυγάτηρ θυγατρός, ἡ	daughter
θυμός θυμοῦ, ὁ	life, spirit; soul, heart, mind
θύω, θύσω, ἔθυσα, τέθυκα, τέθυμαι, ἐτύθην	sacrifice

I

ἴδιος ἰδία ἴδιον	one's own; peculiar, separate, distinct
ἱερός –ά –όν	holy, venerated, divine
ἵημι, ἥσω, ἧκα, -εἷκα, εἷμαι, -εἵθην	put in motion, let go, shoot; (mid.) hasten, rush
ἱκανός –ή –όν	sufficient, enough; competent, able to (+infin.)
ἵνα	in order that (conj. +subj. or opt.); where (rel. adv. +indic.)
ἱππεύς ἱππέως, ὁ	horseman, rider, charioteer
ἵππος ἵππου, ὁ	horse
ἴσος ἴση ἴσον	equal, the same as (+dat.)
ἵστημι στήσω will set, ἔστησα set, caused to stand, 2 aor. ἔστην stood, ἔστηκα stand, plup. εἱστήκη stood, ἐστάθην stood	make to stand, set
ἰσχυρός –ά –όν	strong
ἴσως	equally, probably, perhaps

K

καθίστημι, καταστήσω, κατέστησα, κατέστην, καθέστηκα, plupf. καθειστήκη, κατεστάθην	set down, establish; bring into a certain state, render
καί	and, also, even; καί...καί both... and
καιρός καιροῦ, ὁ	the right time
καίτοι (καί-τοι)	and indeed, and yet
κακός –ή –όν	bad, wicked, cowardly
καλέω, καλῶ, ἐκάλεσα, κέκληκα, κέκλημαι, ἐκλήθην	call, summon
καλός –ή –όν	beautiful, noble, honorable
κἄν (καὶ-ἄν)	even if (+subj.)
κατά	down, down (from or along), throughout, according to; κατὰ γῆν by land; κατὰ φύσιν in accordance with nature; κατ᾽ ἔθνη by nations; καθ ἕνα one by one.
καταλαμβάνω, καταλήψομαι, κατέλαβον, κατείληφα, κατείλημμαι, κατελήφθην	seize, catch up with, arrest, compel
κατασκευάζω, κατασκευάσω, κατεσκεύασα	equip, furnish, make ready

κατηγορέω, κατηγορήσω, κατηγόρησα, κατηγόρηκα, κατηγόρημαι, κατηγορήθην

to speak against, to accuse (+gen.)

κεῖμαι, κείσομαι

to lie, be situated, be laid up in store, be set up, be established or ordained (used as pf. pass. of τίθημι)

κελεύω, κελεύσω, ἐκέλευσα, κεκέλευκα, κεκέλευσμαι, ἐκελεύσθην

order, bid, command (+acc. and infin.)

κεφαλή –ῆς, ἡ

head

κίνδυνος κινδύνου, ὁ

danger

κινέω, κινήσω, ἐκίνησα, κεκίνηκα, κεκίνημαι, ἐκινήθην

set in motion, move, rouse

κοινός –ή –όν

common, shared, mutual

κομίζω, κομιῶ, ἐκόμισα, κεκόμικα, κεκόμισμαι, ἐκομίσθην

take care of, provide for

κόσμος κόσμου, ὁ

order; ornament, decoration, adornment; world, universe

κρατέω, κρατήσω, ἐκράτησα, κεκράτηκα, κεκράτημαι, ἐκρατήθην

be victorious, conquer, rule, surpass, excel (+gen.)

κρείσσων κρεῖσσον

stronger, mightier; better, more excellent (comp. of ἀγαθός)

κρίνω, κρινῶ, ἔκρινα, κέκρικα, κέκριμαι, ἐκρίθην

judge, decide, determine

κτάομαι, κτήσομαι, ἐκτησάμην,   get, gain, acquire
κέκτημαι

κύκλος κύκλου, ὁ   circle, ring, orb, disc,
circular motion

κύριος κυρίου, ὁ   lord, master

κωλύω, κωλύσω, ἐκώλυσα,   hinder, check, prevent
κεκώλυκα, κεκώλυμαι, ἐκωλύθην   (+acc. and infin.)

Λ

λαλέω, λαλήσω, ἐλάλησα,   talk, chatter, babble
λελάληκα, ἐλαλήθην

λαμβάνω, λήψομαι, ἔλαβον, εἴληφα,   take, grasp, seize; receive, get
εἴλημμαι, ἐλήφθην

λαμπρός –ά –όν   bright, brilliant; well-known,
illustrious

λανθάνω, λήσω, ἔλαθον, λέληθα   escape the notice of (+acc. and
nom. participle), be unknown;
(mid. and pass.) forget

λαός λαοῦ, ὁ   the people, folk

λέγω, ἐρῶ, εἶπον, εἴρηκα, λέλεγμαι,   say, speak (of), recount; pick up,
ἐλέχθην and ἐρρήθην   collect, count

λείπω, λείψω, ἔλιπον, λέλοιπα,   leave, abandon
λέλειμμαι, ἐλείφθην

λίθος λίθου, ὁ   stone

λόγος λόγου, ὁ   word, speech, discourse; thought,
reason, account

λοιπός –ή –όν	rest, remaining, rest-of-the
λύω, λύσω, ἔλυσα, λέλυκα, λέλυμαι, ἐλύθην	loosen, unbind, set free; undo, destroy

M

μακρός –ά –όν	long, tall, large, long-lasting
μάλα	very, very much
μάλιστα	most, most of all; (in replies) certainly
μᾶλλον	more, rather; μᾶλλον...ἤ rather than
μανθάνω, μαθήσομαι, ἔμαθον, μεμάθηκα	learn, ascertain
μάρτυς μάρτυρος, ὁ/ἡ	witness
μάχη μάχης, ἡ	battle
μάχομαι, μαχοῦμαι, ἐμαχεσάμην, μεμάχημαι	fight (against) (+dat.)
μέγας μεγάλη μέγα	big, great, powerful
μέγεθος μεγέθους, τό	greatness, size, magnitude
μέλλω, μελλήσω, ἐμέλλησα	(+infin.) think of doing, intend to, be about to
μέν...δέ	on the one hand...on the other hand (often untranslated); μέν (by itself) indeed

μέντοι	however; of course
μένω, μενῶ, ἔμεινα, μεμένηκα	stay, remain, endure, await
μέρος μέρους, τό	part, share
μέσος μέση μέσον	middle, in the middle, moderate; τὸ μέσον midst
μετά	with (+gen.); after (+acc.)
μεταξύ	between
μέχρι	until; (prep.) as far as, up to (+gen.)
μή	not (marks the negative as subjective or conditional); εἰ μή if not, except
μηδέ	and not
μηδείς μηδεμία μηδέν	no one, nothing
μήν	[emphasizes preceding particle]
μήτε...μήτε	neither...nor
μήτηρ μητρός, ἡ	mother
μίγνυμι, μείξω, ἔμειξα, μέμειγμαι, ἐμείχθην	mix, mingle
μικρός –ά –όν	small, little, short
μιμνήσκω, -μνήσω, -έμνησα, pf. μέμνημαι, ἐμνήσθην	remind; (in pf. mid.) remember
μόνον	only
μόνος μόνη μόνον	alone, single

μυρίος μυρία μυρίον

countless; μύριοι 10,000;
μυριάς -άδος ἡ 10,000,
a countless amount

N

ναί

indeed, yes (used in strong affirmation)

ναός (νεώς) ναοῦ (νεώ), ὁ

temple

ναῦς νεώς, ἡ

ship

νέος νέα νέον

young, new, fresh

νῆσος νήσου, ἡ

island

νικάω, νικήσω, ἐνίκησα, νενίκηκα, νενίκημαι, ἐνικήθην

conquer, win

νίκη νίκης, ἡ

victory

νομίζω, νομιῶ, ἐνόμισα, νενόμικα, νενόμισμαι, ἐνομίσθην

think, believe that (+acc. and infin.); hold as a custom, be accustomed to (+infin.)

νόμος νόμου, ὁ

custom, tradition, law

νόσος νόσου, ὁ

disease, sickness

νοῦς (νόος), νοῦ (νόου), ὁ

mind, perception, sense

νῦν, νυνί

now

νύξ νυκτός, ἡ

night

Ξ

ξένος ξένου, ὁ	guest-friend; foreigner, stranger

O

ὁ ἡ τό	the
ὄγδοος –η –ον	eighth
ὅδε ἥδε τόδε	this
ὁδός ὁδοῦ, ἡ	road, way, path
ὅθεν	from where, whence
οἶδα, infin. εἰδέναι, imper. ἴσθι, plupf. used as impf. ᾔδειν	to know (pf. in pres. sense); to know how to (+infin.)
οἰκεῖος οἰκεία οἰκεῖον	domestic, of the house; one's own; fitting, suitable
οἰκέω, οἰκήσω, ᾤκησα, ᾤκηκα, ᾠκήθην	inhabit, occupy
οἰκία οἰκίας, ἡ	building, house, dwelling
οἶκος οἴκου, ὁ	house, home, family
οἴομαι or οἶμαι, οἰήσομαι, impf. ᾤμην, aor. ᾠήθην	think, suppose, imagine (+acc. and infin.)
οἷος οἵα οἷον	such as, of what sort, like, (exclam.) what a!, how! ; οἷός τε (+infin.) fit or able to; οἷόν τε (+infin.) it is possible to
ὀκτώ	eight

ὀλίγος ὀλίγη ὀλίγον	little, small, few
ὅλος ὅλη ὅλον	whole, entire, complete
ὅμοιος ὁμοία ὅμοιον	like, resembling (+dat.)
ὁμολογέω, ὁμολογήσω, ὡμολόγησα, ὡμολόγηκα, ὡμολόγημαι, ὡμολογήθην	agree with, say the same thing as (+dat.)
ὅμως	nevertheless, all the same, notwithstanding
ὄνομα ὀνόματος, τό	name; fame
ὀνομάζω, ὀνομάσω, ὠνόμασα, ὠνόμακα, ὠνόμασμαι, ὠνομάσθην	call by name
ὀξύς ὀξεῖα ὀξύ	sharp, keen, shrill, pungent
ὅπλον ὅπλου, τό	weapon, tool, implement (mostly pl.)
ὅπου	where, wherever
ὅπως	how, as; so that, in order that (+subj. or opt.)
ὁράω, ὄψομαι, 2 aor. εἶδον, ἑόρακα and ἑώρακα, ὤφθην, impf. ἑώρων	see, look (to)
ὀρθός –ή –όν	upright, straight, true, regular
ὁρμάω, ὁρμήσω, ὥρμησα, ὥρμηκα, ὥρμημαι, ὡρμήθην	set in motion, urge on; (intrans.) start, hasten on
ὄρος ὄρους, τό	mountain, hill
ὅς ἥ ὅ	who, which, that

ὅσος ὅση ὅσον	however much; as great as; (in pl.) as many as; ὅσον (adv.) as much as
ὅσπερ ἥπερ ὅπερ	the very one who, the very thing which
ὅστις ἥτις ὅ τι	anyone who, anything which; (in indir. quest.) who, which, what
ὅταν (ὅτε-ἄν)	whenever (+subj.)
ὅτε	when, whenever (+indic. or opt.)
ὅτι	because, that; (with superl.) as... as possible
οὐ, οὐκ, οὐχ	not (with indicative verbs)
οὐδέ	and not, but not, nor; οὐδέ...οὐδέ not even...nor yet
οὐδείς οὐδεμία οὐδέν	no one, nothing
οὐκέτι	no longer, no more
οὐκοῦν	surely then (inviting assent to an inference)
οὖν	therefore, accordingly; at any rate
οὐρανός –οῦ, ὁ	sky, heaven
οὐσία οὐσίας, ἡ	substance, property; essence
οὔτε...οὔτε	neither...nor
οὗτος αὕτη τοῦτο	this, these; μετὰ ταῦτα after this

οὕτως	in this way
ὀφθαλμός –οῦ, ὁ	eye

Π

πάθος πάθους, τό	incident, accident, misfortune, experience; passion, emotion; state, condition
παῖς παιδός, ὁ/ἡ	son, daughter, child; slave
παλαιός –ά –όν	old, ancient
πάλιν	back, backwards; again
πάντως	altogether, in all ways; at any rate
πάνυ	altogether, entirely
παρά	from (+gen.); beside (+dat.); to, to the side of, contrary to (+acc.)
παραδίδωμι, παραδώσω, παρέδωκα, παραδέδωκα, παραδέδομαι, παρεδόθην	transmit, hand over, surrender
παρασκευάζω, παρασκευάσω, παρεσκεύασα	get ready, prepare, provide
πάρειμι	be present, be ready or at hand; (impers.) πάρεστί μοι it depends on me, it is in my power; τὰ παρόντα the present circumstances; τὸ παρόν just now

παρέχω, παρέξω, παρέσχον, παρέσχηκα, impf. παρεῖχον	provide
πᾶς πᾶσα πᾶν	every, all; whole (with article)
πάσχω, πείσομαι, ἔπαθον, πέπονθα	suffer, experience, be affected in a certain way (+adv.)
πατήρ πατρός, ὁ	father
πατρίς πατρίδος, ἡ	fatherland
παύω, παύσω, ἔπαυσα, πέπαυκα, πέπαυμαι, ἐπαύθην	stop, put an end to; (mid.) cease
πείθω, πείσω, ἔπεισα, πέποιθα, πέπεισμαι, ἐπείσθην	persuade, win over; (mid. and pass.) obey, believe in, trust in (+dat.)
πειράω (usually mid. πειράομαι), πειράσομαι, ἐπείρασα, πεπείραμαι, ἐπειράθην	attempt, try, make a trial of (+gen.)
πεμπτός –ή –όν	fifth
πέμπω, πέμψω, ἔπεμψα, πέπομφα, πέπεμμαι, ἐπέμφθην	send
πέντε	five
περ	[enclitic added to pronouns and other particles for emphasis]
περί	around, about; concerning (+gen.)
πίνω, πίομαι, 2 aor. ἔπιον, πέπωκα, -πέπομαι, -επόθην	drink
πίπτω, πεσοῦμαι, ἔπεσον, πέπτωκα	fall, fall down

πιστεύω, πιστεύσω, ἐπίστευσα, πεπίστευκα, πεπίστευμαι, ἐπιστεύθην	trust, rely on, believe in (+dat.)
πίστις πίστεως, ἡ	trust in others, faith; that which gives confidence, assurance, pledge, guarantee
πλεῖστος πλείστη πλεῖστον	most, greatest, largest (superl. of πολύς)
πλέον	more, rather
πλέω, πλεύσομαι, ἔπλευσα, πέπλευκα, πέπλευσμαι, ἐπλεύσθην	sail
πλέων πλέον	more, larger (comp. of πολύς)
πλῆθος πλήθους, τό	mass, throng, crowd
πλήν	(prep.) except (+gen.); (conj.) except that, unless, but
πνεῦμα πνεύματος, τό	wind, breath, spirit
ποιέω, ποιήσω, ἐποίησα, πεποίηκα, πεποίημαι, ἐποιήθην	make, produce, cause, do; (mid.) consider, reckon
ποιητής –οῦ, ὁ	creator, poet
ποῖος ποία ποῖον	what sort of?
πολεμέω, πολεμήσω, ἐπολέμησα, πεπολέμηκα	make war
πολέμιος πολεμία πολέμιον	hostile; οἱ πολέμιοι the enemy
πόλεμος πολέμου, ὁ	war

πόλις πόλεως, ἡ	city, city-state
πολιτεία –ας, ἡ	constitution, citizenship, republic
πολλάκις	often
πολύς πολλή πολύ	much, many; ὡς ἐπὶ τὸ πολύ for the most part
πονηρός –ά –όν	worthless, bad, wicked
πόνος πόνου, ὁ	work, labor; stress, trouble, pain
πορεύω, πορεύσω, ἐπόρευσα, πεπόρευμαι, ἐπορεύθην	carry; (mid. and pass) go, walk, march
ποταμός –οῦ, ὁ	river, stream
πότε	when?
ποτε (enclitic)	at some time, ever, in the world
πότερος ποτέρα πότερον	which of the two? πότερον whether
που	(enclitic) somewhere; I suppose, perhaps (to qualify an assertion)
ποῦ	where
πούς ποδός, ὁ	foot
πρᾶγμα πράγματος, τό	thing; (pl.) circumstances, affairs, business
πρᾶξις πράξεως, ἡ	action, transaction, business
πράσσω, πράξω, ἔπραξα, πέπραχα, πέπραγμαι, ἐπράχθην	do, achieve, accomplish; do or fare in a certain way (+adv.)

πρέσβυς πρέσβεως, ὁ	old man; (pl.) ambassadors
πρίν	before, until
πρό	before, in front of (+gen.)
πρός	from the side of, in the presence of (+gen.); near, at, in addition to (+dat.); to, towards, in relation to (+acc.)
προσήκω προσήξω	belong to, have to do with; be fitting for (+dat.); arrive at; οἱ προσήκοντες relatives; τὰ προσήκοντα duties
προστίθημι, προσθήσω, προσέθηκα, προστέθηκα, προστέθειμαι (but commonly προσκεῖμαι instead), προσετέθην	add; (med.) join
πρόσωπον προσώπου, τό	face, mask, person
πρότερος προτέρα πρότερον	before, earlier; τὸ πρότερον previously, before
πρῶτος πρώτη πρῶτον	first, foremost, earliest; (adv.) τὸ πρῶτον in the first place
πυνθάνομαι, πεύσομαι, 2 aor. ἐπυθόμην, πέπυσμαι	learn, hear, inquire concerning (+gen.)
πῦρ πυρός, τό	fire
πως	(enclitic) somehow, in some way, in any way
πῶς	how?

P

ῥᾴδιος ῥᾳδία ῥᾴδιον | easy

Σ

σαφής σαφές | clear, distinct, plain

σημεῖον σημείου, τό | sign, signal, mark

σκοπέω, σκοπήσω, ἐσκόπησα | look at, watch; look into, consider, examine

σός σή σόν | your, yours (sg.; ὑμέτερος = pl.)

σοφός –ή –όν | wise, clever, skilled

στάδιον σταδίου, τό (pl. στάδια and στάδιοι) | stadion or stade, the longest Greek unit of linear measure, about 185 meters

στόμα στόματος, τό | mouth, face, opening

στρατηγός –οῦ, ὁ | leader of an army, commander, general

στρατιά –ᾶς, ἡ | army

στρατιώτης –ου, ὁ | soldier

στρατός –οῦ, ὁ | army

σύ, σοῦ, (pl.) ὑμεῖς, ὑμῶν | you

συμβαίνω, συμβήσομαι, 2 aor. συνέβην, συμβέβηκα | meet, come to an agreement, correspond; happen, occur, come to pass; turn out in a certain way (+adv.), result

σύμμαχος –ον	allied with (+dat.); οἱ σύμμαχοι allies
συμφέρω, συνοίσω, 1 aor. συνήνεγκα	benefit, be useful or profitable to (+dat.); (impers.) συμφέρει it is of use, expedient (+infin.); τὸ συμφέρον use, profit, advantage
συμφορά –ᾶς, ἡ	event, circumstance, misfortune
σύν	with (+ dat. of accompaniment or means)
σχῆμα σχήματος, τό	form, figure, appearance, character
σῴζω, σώσω, ἔσωσα, σέσωκα, ἐσώθην	save
σῶμα σώματος, τό	body
σωτηρία σωτηρίας, ἡ	safety, deliverance

T

τάξις τάξεως, ἡ	arrangement, order; military unit
τάσσω, τάξω, ἔταξα, τέταχα, τέταγμαι, ἐτάχθην	arrange, put in order
ταχύς ταχεῖα ταχύ	quick, fast; (adv.) τάχα quickly; perhaps
τε	and; τε…τε both…and
τεῖχος τείχους, τό	wall
τέκνον τέκνου, τό	child

τελευτάω, τελευτήσω, ἐτελεύτησα, ἐτελευτήθην	finish; die
τέλος τέλους, τό τετελεύτηκα, τετελεύτημαι	end, fulfillment, achievement
τέμνω, τεμῶ, 2 aor. ἔτεμον, -τέτμηκα, τέτμημαι, ἐτμήθην	cut, cut down, cut to pieces
τέταρτος –η –ον	fourth
τέτταρες τέτταρα	four
τέχνη τέχνης, ἡ	art, skill, craft
τίθημι, θήσω, ἔθηκα, τέθηκα, τέθειμαι (but usu. κεῖμαι instead), ἐτέθην	to put, place; establish, ordain, institute; put in a certain state
τίκτω, τέξω or τέξομαι, ἔτεκον, τέτοκα, τέτεγμαι, ἐτέχθην	beget, give birth to, produce
τιμάω, τιμήσω, ἐτίμησα, τετίμηκα, τετίμημαι, ἐτιμήθην	to honor
τιμή τιμῆς, ἡ	honor, esteem; price, value; office, magistracy
τις τι	someone, something, anyone, anything, some, any (enclitic indef. pron./adj.)
τίς τί	who? what? which? (interrog. pron./adj.)
τοίνυν (τοί-νυν)	therefore, accordingly (inferential); further, moreover (transitional)

τοιόσδε τοιάδε τοιόνδε	such (as this), of such a sort (as this)
τοιοῦτος τοιαύτη τοιοῦτο	such, of such a sort
τολμάω, τολμήσω, ἐτόλμησα, τετόλμηκα, τετόλμημαι, ἐτολμήθην	have the courage, dare; undertake, undergo
τόπος τόπου, ὁ	place; topic
τοσοῦτος –αύτη –οῦτο(ν)	so large, so much
τότε	then, at that time; οἱ τότε the men of that time (opp. οἱ νῦν)
τρεῖς τρία	three
τρέπω, τρέψω, ἔτρεψα, τέτροφα, ἐτράπην	turn, direct towards a thing; put to flight, defeat; (pass.) turn one's steps in a certain direction, go
τρέφω, θρέψω, ἔθρεψα, τέθραμμαι, ἐτράφην	nourish, feed, support, maintain; rear, educate
τριάκοντα	thirty
τριακοστός –ή –όν	thirtieth
τρίτος –η –ον	third
τρόπος τρόπου, ὁ	way, manner, fashion; way of life, habit, custom
τροφή τροφῆς, ἡ	nourishment, food
τυγχάνω, τεύξομαι, ἔτυχον, τετύχηκα. τέτυγμαι, ἐτύχθην	hit, light upon, meet by chance (+gen.); reach, gain, obtain; happen to be (+ptc.)

τύχη τύχης, ἡ	luck, fortune (good or bad), fate, chance

ὕδωρ ὕδατος, τό	water
υἱός υἱοῦ, ὁ	son
ὑμέτερος ὑμετέρα ὑμέτερον	your, yours (pl.; σός = sg.)
ὑπάρχω, ὑπάρξω, ὑπῆρξα, ὑπῆργμαι, ὑπήρχθην	exist, be, belong to; τὰ ὑπάρχοντα existing circumstances
ὑπέρ	for (+gen), beyond (+acc.)
ὑπό	under (+gen., dat.); by (+gen. of personal agent); down under (+acc.)
ὑπολαμβάνω, ὑπολήψομαι, ὑπέλαβον, ὑπείληφα, ὑπείλημμαι, ὑπελήφθην	take up, seize; answer, reply; assume, suppose
ὕστερος ὑστέρα ὕστερον	coming after, following (+gen.); next, later; (adv.) ὕστερον afterwards

Φ

φαίνω, φανῶ, ἔφηνα, πέφηνα, πέφασμαι, ἐφάνην
bring to light, make appear, make clear; (pass.) come to light, be seen, appear, appear to be (+ptc. or infin.)

φανερός –ά –όν
clear, evident

φέρω, οἴσω, 1 aor. ἤνεγκα, 2 aor. ἤνεγκον, ἐνήνοχα, ἐνήνεγμαι, ἠνέχθην
carry, bring, fetch; carry off or away; φέρε come now, well

φεύγω, φεύξομαι, ἔφυγον, πέφευγα
flee, run away, avoid, shun

φημί, φήσω, impf. ἔφην
say, assert, declare; οὐ φημί deny, refuse, say that...not

φίλος φίλη φίλον
beloved, dear; friendly

φοβέω, φοβήσω, ἐφόβησα, πεφόβημαι, ἐφοβήθην
put to flight; (mid. and pass.) flee, fear

φόβος φόβου, ὁ
panic, fear, flight

φράζω, φράσω, ἔφρασα, πέφρακα, πέφρασμαι, ἐφράσθην
tell, declare; (mid. and pass.) think (about)

φρονέω, φρονήσω, ἐφρόνησα
think, intend to (+infin.); be minded towards (+adv. and dat.)

φυλάσσω, φυλάξω, ἐφύλαξα, πεφύλαχα, πεφύλαγμαι, ἐφυλάχθην
watch, guard, defend; (mid.) be on one's guard against (+acc.)

φύσις φύσεως, ἡ
nature; (of the mind) one's nature or disposition; regular order of nature

φύω, φύσω, ἔφυσα	bring forth, produce, beget; 2 aor. ἔφυν grew, pf. πέφυκα be by nature
φωνή φωνῆς, ἡ	sound, voice
φῶς φωτός, τό	light, daylight

X

χαίρω, χαιρήσω, κεχάρηκα, κεχάρημαι, ἐχάρην	to be happy, rejoice at (+dat.), take joy in (+ptc.); χαῖρε, (pl.) χαίρετε hello, goodbye
χαλεπός –ή –όν	difficult, troublesome
χαλκοῦς –ῆ –οῦν	of copper or bronze
χάρις χάριτος, ἡ	splendor, honor, glory; favor, goodwill, gratitude, thanks
χείρ χειρός, ἡ	hand
χείρων χεῖρον	worse, inferior (comp. of κακός)
χράομαι, χρήσομαι, ἐχρησάμην, κέχρημαι, ἐχρήσθην	use, experience, suffer (+dat.); treat someone in a certain way (+dat. and adv.)
χρή, impf. χρῆν or ἐχρῆν, infin. χρῆναι	it is necessary, it is fated, one ought (+infin. or +acc. and infin.)
χρῆμα χρήματος, τό	thing, matter; (more commonly in pl.) goods or property, esp. money
χρήσιμος χρησίμη χρήσιμον	useful, serviceable

χρόνος χρόνου, ὁ	time
χώρα χώρας, ἡ	land; place
χωρίον χωρίου, τό	place, spot, district
χωρίς	separately, apart; (+gen.) without, separate from

Ψ

ψυχή ψυχῆς, ἡ	breath, life, soul

Ω

ὦ	oh! (unemphatic when with the vocative)
ὧδε	thus, in this way; hither, here
ὡς	as, since; (introducing purpose clause) so that (+subj./opt.); (introducing indir. statement) that
ὥσπερ	just as, as if
ὥστε	(introducing natural or actual result clause) so as, so that, (with the result) that

1-50

ὁ ἡ τό	the
αὐτός αὐτή αὐτό	him- her- itself etc. (for emphasis); the same (with article); (pron.) him, her, it etc. (in oblique cases)
καί	and, also, even; καί...καί both... and
δέ	and; but
τίς τί	who? what? which? (interrog. pron./adj.)
εἰμί, ἔσομαι, impf. ἦν, infin. εἶναι	be, exist
οὗτος αὕτη τοῦτο	this, these; μετὰ ταῦτα after this
ἤ	or; than (after a comparative); ἤ...ἤ either...or
ἐν	in, among (+dat.)
μέν...δέ	on the one hand...on the other hand (often untranslated); μέν (by itself) indeed
τις τι	someone, something, anyone, anything, some, any (enclitic indef. pron./adj.)
ὅς ἥ ὅ	who, which, that
γάρ	for (explanatory), indeed, in fact (confirming)
οὐ, οὐκ, οὐχ	not (with indicative verbs)
λέγω, ἐρῶ, εἶπον, εἴρηκα, λέλεγμαι, ἐλέχθην and ἐρρήθην	say, speak (of), recount; pick up, collect, count

GREEK: Frequency Listing

ὡς	as, since; (introducing purpose clause) so that (+subj./opt.); (introducing indir. statement) that
τε	and; τε...τε both...and
εἰς	into, to, towards (+acc.)
ἐπί	at (+gen.); on (+dat.); on to, against (+acc.)
κατά	down, down (from or along), throughout, according to; κατὰ γῆν by land; κατὰ φύσιν in accordance with nature; κατ' ἔθνη by nations; καθ'→ἕνα one by one.
ἐγώ ἐμοῦ, (pl.) ἡμεῖς, ἡμῶν	I, we
πρός	from the side of, in the presence of (+gen.); near, at, in addition to (+dat.); to, towards, in relation to (+acc.)
γίγνομαι, γενήσομαι, 2 aor. ἐγενόμην, γέγονα, γεγένημαι, ἐγενήθην	become; be born; happen, be
ἐάν (εἰ-ἄν)	if (+subj.)
διά	through, during, because of (+gen., acc.)
ἀλλά	but
πᾶς πᾶσα πᾶν	every, all; whole (with article)
ἔχω, ἕξω or σχήσω, 2 aor. ἔσχον, ἔσχηκα, impf. εἶχον	have, hold, keep
ἐκ, ἐξ	from, out of (+gen.)

πολύς πολλή πολύ	much, many; ὡς ἐπὶ τὸ πολύ for the most part
περί	around, about; concerning (+gen.)
μή	not (marks the negative as subjective or conditional); εἰ μή if not, except
ὅστις ἥτις ὅ τι	anyone who, anything which; (in indir. quest.) who, which, what
ἄν	[marks verbs as potential (with optative), or generalizing (with subjunctive)]
σύ, σοῦ, (pl.) ὑμεῖς, ὑμῶν	you
ἀνά	up, on; throughout
ὅτι	because, that; (with superl.) as... as possible
εἰ	if (+indic. or opt.); εἴπερ if indeed
ἄλλος ἄλλη ἄλλο	other, another
ἀπό	from (+gen.)
φημί, φήσω, impf. ἔφην	say, assert, declare; οὐ φημί deny, refuse, say that...not
ὑπό	under (+gen., dat.); by (+gen. of personal agent); down under (+acc.)
ποιέω, ποιήσω, ἐποίησα, πεποίηκα, πεποίημαι, ἐποιήθην	make, produce, cause, do; (mid.) consider, reckon
οὖν	therefore, accordingly; at any rate
λόγος λόγου, ὁ	word, speech, discourse; thought, reason, account

παρά	from (+gen.); beside (+dat.); to, to the side of, contrary to (+acc.)
οὕτως	in this way
πρότερος προτέρα πρότερον	before, earlier; τὸ πρότερον previously, before
θεός θεοῦ, ὁ/ἡ	god, goddess

51-100

μετά	with (+gen.); after (+acc.)
ἑαυτοῦ ἑαυτῆς ἑαυτοῦ	him- her- itself (reflexive pron.)
μέγας μεγάλη μέγα	big, great, powerful
οὐδέ	and not, but not, nor; οὐδέ...οὐδέ not even...nor yet
ἐκεῖνος ἐκείνη ἐκεῖνο	that person or thing; ἐκεῖνος... οὗτος the former...the latter
τοιοῦτος τοιαύτη τοιοῦτο	such, of such a sort
οὐδείς οὐδεμία οὐδέν	no one, nothing
εἶπον	I said, I spoke, 2 aor. λέγω, φημί
ἀγαθός –ή –όν	good, virtuous, brave, noble
γε	(enclitic) indeed; at least, at any rate
δή	surely, really, now, in fact, indeed (gives greater exactness)
πόλις πόλεως, ἡ	city, city-state
εἷς μία ἕν	one

ἵημι, ἥσω, ἧκα, -εἷκα, εἷμαι, -εἵθην

put in motion, let go, shoot; (mid.) hasten, rush

δέω, δεήσω, ἐδέησα, δεδέηκα, δεδέημαι, ἐδεήθην

lack, miss, stand in need of (+gen.)

ἄνθρωπος –ου, ὁ/ἡ

human being

ὁράω, ὄψομαι, 2 aor. εἶδον, ἑόρακα and ἑώρακα, ὤφθην, impf. ἑώρων

see, look (to)

μόνος μόνη μόνον

alone, single

οὔτε...οὔτε

neither...nor

οἷος οἵα οἷον

such as, of what sort, like, (exclam.) what a!, how! ; οἷός τε (+infin.) fit or able to; οἷόν τε (+infin.) it is possible to

λαμβάνω, λήψομαι, ἔλαβον, εἴληφα, εἴλημμαι, ἐλήφθην

take, grasp, seize; receive, get

δοκέω, δόξω, ἔδοξα

think, suppose, imagine (+acc. and infin.); seem, seem good; (impers.) δοκεῖ μοι it seems to me

ἕτερος ἑτέρα ἕτερον

the other (of two); other, another

κακός –ή –όν

bad, wicked, cowardly

ἀνήρ ἀνδρός, ὁ

man, husband

ἐπεί

after, since, when

ὅσος ὅση ὅσον

however much; as great as; (in pl.) as many as; ὅσον (adv.) as much as

καλέω, καλῶ, ἐκάλεσα, κέκληκα, κέκλημαι, ἐκλήθην

call, summon

σῶμα σώματος, τό

body

δεῖ, δεήσει, impf. ἔδει	it is necessary, one must, one ought (+acc. and infin.)
ὥσπερ	just as, as if
δίδωμι, δώσω, ἔδωκα, δέδωκα, δέδομαι, ἐδόθην	give, grant, offer
ἔτι	still, yet
φύσις φύσεως, ἡ	nature; (of the mind) one's nature or disposition; regular order of nature
μικρός –ά –όν	small, little, short
δύναμαι, δυνήσομαι, ἐδυνήθην, δεδύνημαι	(+infin.) to be able (to), be strong enough (to)
ὥστε	(introducing natural or actual result clause) so as, so that, (with the result) that
ἀρχή ἀρχῆς, ἡ	beginning, origin; rule, empire, realm; magistracy
ἕκαστος ἑκάστη ἕκαστον	each (of several)
ἡμέρα ἡμέρας, ἡ	day
φύω, φύσω, ἔφυσα	bring forth, produce, beget; 2 aor. ἔφυν grew, pf. πέφυκα be by nature
ἅπας ἅπασα ἅπαν	all together
ὅμοιος ὁμοία ὅμοιον	like, resembling (+dat.)
νῦν, νυνί	now
γῆ γῆς, ἡ	earth
δύναμις δυνάμεως, ἡ	power, strength, ability

καλός –ή –όν	beautiful, noble, honorable
κύριος κυρίου, ὁ	lord, master
μᾶλλον	more, rather; μᾶλλον...ἤ rather than
ὅδε ἥδε τόδε	this

101-150

ὅλος ὅλη ὅλον	whole, entire, complete
μέρος μέρους, τό	part, share
ἄρα	therefore, then (drawing an inference)
ἐμός ἐμή ἐμόν	my, mine
χράομαι, χρήσομαι, ἐχρησάμην, κέχρημαι, ἐχρήσθην	use, experience, suffer (+dat.); treat someone in a certain way (+dat. and adv.)
δύο	two
χρόνος χρόνου, ὁ	time
ἴσος ἴση ἴσον	equal, the same as (+dat.)
ὅταν (ὅτε-ἄν)	whenever (+subj.)
μόνον	only
οἶδα, infin. εἰδέναι, imper. ἴσθι,	to know (pf. in pres. sense); plupf. used as impf. ᾔδειν to know how to (+infin.)
βασιλεύς βασιλέως, ὁ	king
ὦ	oh! (unemphatic when with the vocative)

βούλομαι, βουλήσομαι, βεβούλημαι, ἐβουλήθην — (+infin.) will, wish (to); be willing (to); ὁ βουλόμενος anyone who likes

φαίνω, φανῶ, ἔφηνα, πέφηνα, πέφασμαι, ἐφάνην — bring to light, make appear, make clear; (pass.) come to light, be seen, appear, appear to be (+ptc. or infin.)

γράφω, γράψω, ἔγραψα, γέγραφα, γέγραμμαι, ἐγράφην — write

φέρω, οἴσω, 1 aor. ἤνεγκα, 2 aor. ἤνεγκον, ἐνήνοχα, ἐνήνεγμαι, ἠνέχθην — carry, bring, fetch; carry off or away; φέρε come now, well

ψυχή ψυχῆς, ἡ — breath, life, soul

μηδείς μηδεμία μηδέν — no one, nothing

αἴτιος αἰτία αἴτιον — responsible, guilty

πάλιν — back, backwards; again

μάλιστα — most, most of all; (in replies) certainly

ὑπάρχω, ὑπάρξω, ὑπῆρξα, ὑπῆργμαι, ὑπήρχθην — exist, be, belong to; τὰ ὑπάρχοντα existing circumstances

ἄρχω, ἄρξω, ἦρξα, ἦργμαι, ἤρχθην — begin (+gen.); lead, rule, govern (+gen.)

γυνή γυναικός, ἡ — woman, wife

ποτε (enclitic) — at some time, ever, in the world

ἵνα — in order that (conj. +subj. or opt.); where (rel. adv. +indic.)

ὄνομα ὀνόματος, τό — name; fame

ὑπέρ — for (+gen), beyond (+acc.)

ἤδη	already, now (of the immediate past); presently (of the immediate future)
πατήρ πατρός, ὁ	father
ἀκούω, ἀκούσομαι, ἤκουσα, ἀκήκοα, plup. ἠκηκόη or ἀκηκόη, ἠκούσθην	listen (to), hear (of)
γένος γένους, τό	race, family; kind, class
τόπος τόπου, ὁ	place; topic
πράσσω, πράξω, ἔπραξα, πέπραχα, πέπραγμαι, ἐπράχθην	do, achieve, accomplish; do or fare in a certain way (+adv.)
πρῶτος πρώτη πρῶτον	first, foremost, earliest; (adv.) τὸ πρῶτον in the first place
εὑρίσκω, εὑρήσω, 2 aor. ηὗρον or εὗρον, ηὕρηκα or εὕρηκα, εὕρημαι, εὑρέθην	find (out), discover, devise
παῖς παιδός, ὁ/ἡ	son, daughter, child; slave
ἔρχομαι, fut. εἶμι or ἐλεύσομαι, 2 aor. ἦλθον, ἐλήλυθα	come, go
υἱός υἱοῦ, ὁ	son
ὕδωρ ὕδατος, τό	water
ἴδιος ἰδία ἴδιον	one's own; peculiar, separate, distinct
σός σή σόν	your, yours (sg.; ὑμέτερος = pl.)
γιγνώσκω, γνώσομαι, ἔγνων, ἔγνωκα, ἔγνωσμαι, ἐγνώσθην	come to know, learn; judge, think, or determine that (+acc. and infin.)
τυγχάνω, τεύξομαι, ἔτυχον, τετύχηκα. τέτυγμαι, ἐτύχθην	hit, light upon, meet by chance (+gen.); reach, gain, obtain; happen to be (+ptc.)

ἵστημι στήσω will set, ἔστησα set,
caused to stand, 2 aor. ἔστην stood,
ἔστηκα stand, plup. εἱστήκη stood,
ἐστάθην stood | make to stand, set

ἅμα | at the same time; (prep.) together with (+dat.)

ἄγω, ἄξω, ἤγαγον, ἦχα, ἦγμαι, ἤχθην | lead, carry, bring; pass (time)

τρόπος τρόπου, ὁ | way, manner, fashion; way of life, habit, custom

μήτε...μήτε | neither...nor

151-200

μέσος μέση μέσον | middle, in the middle, moderate; τὸ μέσον midst

ἀλλήλων –οις | (oblique cases plural only) one another, each other

ἀεί | always

φίλος φίλη φίλον | beloved, dear; friendly

συμβαίνω, συμβήσομαι, 2 aor. συνέβην, συμβέβηκα | meet, come to an agreement, correspond; happen, occur, come to pass; turn out in a certain way (+adv.), result

ἔργον ἔργου, τό | work, achievement, exploit

πλέω, πλεύσομαι, ἔπλευσα, πέπλευκα, πέπλευσμαι, ἐπλεύσθην | sail

τότε | then, at that time; οἱ τότε the men of that time (opp. οἱ νῦν)

μήν | [emphasizes preceding particle]

GREEK: Frequency Listing

χρή, impf. χρῆν or ἐχρῆν, infin. χρῆναι	it is necessary, it is fated, one ought (+infin. or +acc. and infin.)
δείκνυμι, δείξω, ἔδειξα, δέδειχα, δέδειγμαι, ἐδείχθην	show, point out
ζῷον ζῴου, τό	living being, animal
πρᾶγμα πράγματος, τό	thing; (pl.) circumstances, affairs, business
ἐναντίος ἐναντία ἐναντίον	opposite, facing; opposing
τίθημι, θήσω, ἔθηκα, τέθηκα, τέθειμαι (but usu. κεῖμαι instead), ἐτέθην	to put, place; establish, ordain, institute; put in a certain state
εἶδον, 2 aor. of ὁράω, act. infin. ἰδεῖν, mid.infin. ἰδέσθαι	I saw
χείρ χειρός, ἡ	hand
μηδέ	and not
ὀλίγος ὀλίγη ὀλίγον	little, small, few
νόμος νόμου, ὁ	custom, tradition, law
κοινός –ή –όν	common, shared, mutual
οἴομαι or οἶμαι, οἰήσομαι, impf. ᾤμην, aor. ᾠήθην	think, suppose, imagine (+acc. and infin.)
κινέω, κινήσω, ἐκίνησα, κεκίνηκα, κεκίνημαι, ἐκινήθην	set in motion, move, rouse
πάσχω, πείσομαι, ἔπαθον, πέπονθα	suffer, experience, be affected in a certain way (+adv.)
πῶς	how?
ὅσπερ ἥπερ ὅπερ	the very one who, the very thing which

τοσοῦτος –αύτη –οῦτο(ν)	so large, so much
σύν	with (+ dat. of accompaniment or means)
εἶτα	then, next
ἀληθής –ές	true
δίκαιος δικαία δίκαιον	right, just
μέλλω, μελλήσω, ἐμέλλησα	(+infin.) think of doing, intend to, be about to
ἐθέλω, ἐθελήσω, ἠθέλησα, ἠθέληκα	(+infin.) wish (to); be willing (to)
λοιπός –ή –όν	rest, remaining, rest-of-the
ἀνάγκη ἀνάγκης, ἡ	necessity
ὅτε	when, whenever (+indic. or opt.)
δεύτερος –α –ον	second
πόλεμος πολέμου ὁ	war
χώρα χώρας, ἡ	land; place
ζάω, ζήσω, ἔζησα, ἔζηκα	live
πλῆθος πλήθους, τό	mass, throng, crowd
ἥλιος ἡλίου, ὁ	sun
αἰτία αἰτίας, ἡ	cause, origin; charge, accusation
πείθω, πείσω, ἔπεισα, πέποιθα, πέπεισμαι, ἐπείσθην	persuade, win over; (mid. and pass.) obey, believe in, trust in (+dat.)

πάρειμι	be present, be ready or at hand; (impers.) πάρεστί μοι it depends on me, it is in my power; τὰ παρόντα the present circumstances; τὸ παρόν just now
πλεῖστος πλείστη πλεῖστον	most, greatest, largest (superl. of πολύς)
εἶδος εἴδους, τό	form, shape, figure; class, kind, sort
ὅπως	how, as; so that, in order that (+subj. or opt.)
τρεῖς τρία	three
βίος βίου, ὁ	life

201-250

νομίζω, νομιῶ, ἐνόμισα, νενόμικα, νενόμισμαι, ἐνομίσθην	think, believe that (+acc. and infin.); hold as a custom, be accustomed to (+infin.)
κύκλος κύκλου, ὁ	circle, ring, orb, disc, circular motion
πάθος πάθους, τό	incident, accident, misfortune, experience; passion, emotion; state, condition
πρό	before, in front of (+gen.)
ὀνομάζω, ὀνομάσω, ὠνόμασα, ὠνόμακα, ὠνόμασμαι, ὠνομάσθην	call by name
μέντοι	however; of course
ἀρετή ἀρετῆς, ἡ	goodness, excellence; virtue; valor, bravery

ὑμέτερος ὑμετέρα ὑμέτερον	your, yours (pl.; σός = sg.)
ἔτος ἔτους, τό	year
ἀντί	opposite (+gen.)
ναῦς νεώς, ἡ	ship
τρίτος –η –ον	third
πνεῦμα πνεύματος, τό	wind, breath, spirit
ὀρθός –ή –όν	upright, straight, true, regular
θάλασσα θαλάσσης, ἡ	the sea
διαφέρω, διοίσω, 1 aor. διήνεγκα, 2 aor. διήνεγκον, διενήνοχα, διενήνεγμαι	carry in different ways, spread; differ; (impers.) διαφέρει it makes a difference to (+dat.)
μέχρι	until; (prep.) as far as, up to (+gen.)
δόξα δόξης, ἡ	opinion, judgment; reputation, honor, glory
κεφαλή –ῆς, ἡ	head
πῦρ πυρός, τό	fire
ἐλάσσων ἔλασσον	smaller, less, fewer (comp. of μικρός)
πούς ποδός, ὁ	foot
ἱερός –ά –όν	holy, venerated, divine
εὐθύς εὐθεῖα εὐθύ	straight, direct; (adv.) immediately
εἶμι, infin. ἰέναι, ptc. ἰών, ἰοῦσα, ἰόν	I will go (fut. of ἔρχομαι)
ταχύς ταχεῖα ταχύ	quick, fast; (adv.) τάχα quickly; perhaps

ποταμός –οῦ, ὁ	river, stream
οὐσία οὐσίας, ἡ	substance, property; essence
ἀριθμός –οῦ, ὁ	number
ὕστερος ὑστέρα ὕστερον	coming after, following (+gen.); next, later; (adv.) ὕστερον afterwards
φυλάσσω, φυλάξω, ἐφύλαξα, πεφύλαχα, πεφύλαγμαι, ἐφυλάχθην	watch, guard, defend; (mid.) be on one's guard against (+acc.)
καιρός καιροῦ, ὁ	the right time
οἰκέω, οἰκήσω, ᾤκησα, ᾤκηκα, ᾠκήθην	inhabit, occupy
ἀμφότερος ἀμφοτέρα ἀμφότερον	both
σημεῖον σημείου, τό	sign, signal, mark
παρέχω, παρέξω, παρέσχον, παρέσχηκα, impf. παρεῖχον	provide
ἑκάτερος ἑκατέρα ἑκάτερον	each (of two)
δηλόω, δηλώσω, ἐδήλωσα, δεδήλωκα, ἐδηλώθην	show, declare, explain
οἰκεῖος οἰκεία οἰκεῖον	domestic, of the house; one's own; fitting, suitable
κελεύω, κελεύσω, ἐκέλευσα, κεκέλευκα, κεκέλευσμαι, ἐκελεύσθην	order, bid, command (+acc. and infin.)
τέλος τέλους, τό	end, fulfillment, achievement
ἡγέομαι, ἡγήσομαι, ἡγησάμην, ἥγημαι	lead, be the leader; regard, believe, think
ἄξιος ἀξία ἄξιον	worthy, deserving
ἦ	truly (emphasizes what follows)

δῆλος δήλη δῆλον	visible, clear, manifest
τοίνυν (τοί-νυν)	therefore, accordingly (inferential); further, moreover (transitional)
πολέμιος πολεμία πολέμιον	hostile; οἱ πολέμιοι the enemy
ἔρομαι, ἐρήσομαι, 2 aor. ἠρόμην	ask, ask one about (+double acc.)
ἀδελφός –οῦ, ὁ	brother
μέγεθος μεγέθους, τό	greatness, size, magnitude

251-300

εἴτε...εἴτε	whether...or
κεῖμαι, κείσομαι	to lie, be situated, be laid up in store, be set up, be established or ordained (used as pf. pass. of τίθημι)
πολλάκις	often
πίνω, πίομαι, 2 aor. ἔπιον, πέπωκα, -πέπομαι, -επόθην	drink
χάρις χάριτος, ἡ	splendor, honor, glory; favor, goodwill, gratitude, thanks
ἔπειτα	then, next
ζητέω, ζητήσω, ἐζήτησα, ἐζήτηκα	seek
σχῆμα σχήματος, τό	form, figure, appearance, character
τροφή τροφῆς, ἡ	nourishment, food
μανθάνω, μαθήσομαι, ἔμαθον, μεμάθηκα	learn, ascertain

ἐνταῦθα	here, there
φεύγω, φεύξομαι, ἔφυγον, πέφευγα	flee, run away, avoid, shun
ἵππος ἵππου, ὁ	horse
κόσμος κόσμου, ὁ	order; ornament, decoration, adornment; world, universe
αἷμα αἵματος, τό	blood
αἱρέω, αἱρήσω, 2 aor. εἷλον, ᾕρηκα, ᾕρημαι, ᾑρέθην	take, grasp, take by force; (mid.) choose
προστίθημι, προσθήσω, προσέθηκα, προστέθηκα, προστέθειμαι (but commonly προσκεῖμαι instead), προσετέθην	add; (med.) join
ἀξιόω, ἀξιώσω, ἠξίωσα, ἠξίωκα, ἠξίωμαι, ἠξιώθην	consider worthy
ἕως	until; while, so long as
νέος νέα νέον	young, new, fresh
ἔοικα, ptc. εἰκώς	be like, look like (+dat.); seem; befit
κἄν (καὶ-ἄν)	even if (+subj.)
καθίστημι, καταστήσω, κατέστησα, κατέστην, καθέστηκα, plupf. καθειστήκη, κατεστάθην	set down, establish; bring into a certain state, render
τέχνη τέχνης, ἡ	art, skill, craft
χρῆμα χρήματος, τό	thing, matter; (more commonly in pl.) goods or property, esp. money
σῴζω, σώσω, ἔσωσα, σέσωκα, ἐσώθην	save

πέμπω, πέμψω, ἔπεμψα, πέπομφα, πέπεμμαι, ἐπέμφθην	send
φωνή φωνῆς, ἡ	sound, voice
ἕνεκα	on account of, for the sake of (+gen.)
ἀπόλλυμι, ἀπολῶ, ἀπώλεσα, 2 aor. mid. ἀπωλόμην, pf. ἀπολώλεκα ("I have utterly destroyed") or ἀπόλωλα ("I am undone")	kill, destroy; (mid.) perish, die
θάνατος θανάτου, ὁ	death
νύξ νυκτός, ἡ	night
ὁδός ὁδοῦ, ἡ	road, way, path
ἔθνος ἔθνους, τό	nation
ἀποδίδωμι, ἀποδώσω, ἀπέδωκα, ἀποδέδωκα, ἀποδέδομαι, ἀπεδόθην	give back; render; allow; (mid.) sell
νοῦς (νόος), νοῦ (νόου), ὁ	mind, perception, sense
μένω, μενῶ, ἔμεινα, μεμένηκα	stay, remain, endure, await
ἀποθνῄσκω, ἀποθανοῦμαι, 2 aor. ἀπέθανον, ἀποτέθνηκα	die
πάνυ	altogether, entirely
εὖ	well (opp. κακῶς); thoroughly, competently; happily, fortunately
κρίνω, κρινῶ, ἔκρινα, κέκρικα, κέκριμαι, ἐκρίθην	judge, decide, determine
ἀναιρέω, ἀναιρήσω, ἀνεῖλον, ἀνῄρηκα, ἀνῄρημαι, ἀνῃρέθην	raise, take up; kill, destroy

μακρός –ά –όν	long, tall, large, long-lasting
ἥκω, ἥξω, pf. ἥκα	I have come, I am present
ἡδονή –ῆς, ἡ	pleasure, enjoyment
μήτηρ μητρός, ἡ	mother
δεινός –ή –όν	awesome, terrible; clever, clever at (+infin.)
διαφορά –ᾶς, ἡ	difference, disagreement
κρατέω, κρατήσω, ἐκράτησα, κεκράτηκα, κεκράτημαι, ἐκρατήθην	be victorious, conquer, rule, surpass, excel (+gen.)
δῆμος δήμου, ὁ	the (common) people; country district (opp. πόλις)

301-350

οὐρανός –οῦ, ὁ	sky, heaven
ἕπομαι ἕψομαι, 2 aor. ἑσπόμην	follow
ἥσσων ἧσσον	less, weaker (comp. of κακός or μικρός)
ὄρος ὄρους, τό	mountain, hill
πλήν	(prep.) except (+gen.); (conj.) except that, unless, but
τέτταρες τέτταρα	four
δυνατός –ή –όν	strong, powerful, able
οἶκος οἴκου, ὁ	house, home, family
ἄριστος ἀρίστη ἄριστον	best, noblest (superl. of ἀγαθός)
ῥᾴδιος ῥᾳδία ῥᾴδιον	easy

ἀφαιρέω, ἀφαιρήσω, ἀφεῖλον, ἀφήρηκα, ἀφήρημαι, ἀφηρέθην	take from, take away
τύχη τύχης, ἡ	luck, fortune (good or bad), fate, chance
φανερός –ά –όν	clear, evident
πρόσωπον προσώπου, τό	face, mask, person
πιστεύω, πιστεύσω, ἐπίστευσα, πεπίστευκα, πεπίστευμαι, ἐπιστεύθην	trust, rely on, believe in (+dat.)
διδάσκω, διδάξω, ἐδίδαξα, δεδίδαχα, δεδίδαγμαι, ἐδιδάχθην	teach
ἄνω	up, upwards
τάσσω, τάξω, ἔταξα, τέταχα, τέταγμαι, ἐτάχθην	arrange, put in order
ὀφθαλμός –οῦ, ὁ	eye
δέχομαι, δέξομαι, ἐδεξάμην, δέδεγμαι, -εδέχθην	take, accept; welcome, entertain
ἀφικνέομαι, ἀφίξομαι, 2 aor. ἀφικόμην, ἀφῖγμαι	come to, arrive at
ἱκανός –ή –όν	sufficient, enough; competent, able to (+infin.)
ἐργάζομαι, ἐργάσομαι, εἰργασάμην, εἴργασμαι	work, labor
μάχη μάχης, ἡ	battle
τρέφω, θρέψω, ἔθρεψα, τέθραμμαι, ἐτράφην	nourish, feed, support, maintain; rear, educate
ἀδύνατος –ον	impossible; powerless
ἀκριβής –ές	exact, accurate, precise

που	(enclitic) somewhere; I suppose, perhaps (to qualify an assertion)
ὅθεν	from where, whence
στόμα στόματος, τό	mouth, face, opening
χωρίς	separately, apart; (+gen.) without, separate from
κρείσσων κρεῖσσον	stronger, mightier; better, more excellent (comp. of ἀγαθός)
βραχύς βραχεῖα βραχύ	brief, short
ἰσχυρός –ά –όν	strong
ἀλήθεια ἀληθείας, ἡ	truth
δίκη δίκης, ἡ	justice, lawsuit, trial, penalty
χωρίον χωρίου, τό	place, spot, district
ἡδύς ἡδεῖα ἡδύ	sweet, pleasant
νόσος νόσου, ὁ	disease, sickness
λίθος λίθου, ὁ	stone
παλαιός –ά –όν	old, ancient
ἀφίημι, ἀφήσω, ἀφῆκα, ἀφεῖκα, ἀφεῖμαι, ἀφείθην	send away, let go; let alone, neglect
ἄλλως	otherwise
πρᾶξις πράξεως, ἡ	action, transaction, business
σαφής σαφές	clear, distinct, plain
σοφός –ή –όν	wise, clever, skilled
νικάω, νικήσω, ἐνίκησα, νενίκηκα, νενίκημαι, ἐνικήθην	conquer, win

ὁμολογέω, ὁμολογήσω, ὡμολόγησα, ὡμολόγηκα, ὡμολόγημαι, ὡμολογήθην	agree with, say the same thing as (+dat.)
ναός (νεώς) ναοῦ (νεώ), ὁ	temple
αὖ, αὖθις	in turn, then, furthermore, again

351-400

πατρίς πατρίδος, ἡ	fatherland
ὀξύς ὀξεῖα ὀξύ	sharp, keen, shrill, pungent
καίτοι (καί-τοι)	and indeed, and yet
πλέον	more, rather
πλέων πλέον	more, larger (comp. of πολύς)
γνώμη γνώμης, ἡ	thought, intelligence, opinion, purpose
τιμή τιμῆς, ἡ	honor, esteem; price, value; office, magistracy
μεταξύ	between
προσήκω προσήξω	belong to, have to do with; be fitting for (+dat.); arrive at; οἱ προσήκοντες relatives; τὰ προσήκοντα duties
πρίν	before, until
ἀδικέω, ἀδικήσω, ἠδίκησα, ἠδίκηκα, ἠδίκημαι, ἠδικήθην	do wrong; injure
στρατηγός –οῦ, ὁ	leader of an army, commander, general
οὐκέτι	no longer, no more

πρέσβυς πρέσβεως, ὁ	old man; (pl.) ambassadors
παύω, παύσω, ἔπαυσα, πέπαυκα, πέπαυμαι, ἐπαύθην	stop, put an end to; (mid.) cease
τελευτάω, τελευτήσω, ἐτελεύτησα, τετελεύτηκα, τετελεύτημαι, ἐτελευτήθην	finish; die
μίγνυμι, μείξω, ἔμειξα, μέμειγμαι, ἐμείχθην	mix, mingle
λαός λαοῦ, ὁ	the people, folk
θυγάτηρ θυγατρός, ἡ	daughter
οἰκία οἰκίας, ἡ	building, house, dwelling
παραδίδωμι, παραδώσω, παρέδωκα, παραδέδωκα, παραδέδομαι, παρεδόθην	transmit, hand over, surrender
ἔξω	outside; except
νῆσος νήσου, ἡ	island
ἐκεῖ	there
ἐπιστήμη –ης, ἡ	knowledge, understanding, skill
ἐάω, ἐάσω, εἴασα	allow, permit (+acc. and infin.); let be, let alone
θαυμάζω, θαυμάσομαι, ἐθαύμασα, τεθαύμακα, τεθαύμασμαι, ἐθαυμάσθην	to be in awe (of), be astonished (at)
αἰσθάνομαι, αἰσθήσομαι, 2 aor. ἠσθόμην, ἤσθημαι	perceive, understand, hear, learn
χαίρω, χαιρήσω, κεχάρηκα, κεχάρημαι, ἐχάρην	to be happy, rejoice at (+dat.), take joy in (+ptc.); χαῖρε, (pl.) χαίρετε hello, goodbye

χαλεπός –ή –όν	difficult, troublesome
τέκνον τέκνου, τό	child
καταλαμβάνω, καταλήψομαι, κατέλαβον, κατείληφα, κατείλημμαι, κατελήφθην	seize, catch up with, arrest, compel
μάχομαι, μαχοῦμαι, ἐμαχεσάμην, μεμάχημαι	fight (against) (+dat.)
μιμνήσκω, -μνήσω, -έμνησα, pf. μέμνημαι, ἐμνήσθην	remind; (in pf. mid.) remember
λύω, λύσω, ἔλυσα, λέλυκα, λέλυμαι, ἐλύθην	loosen, unbind, set free; undo, destroy
θνήσκω, 2 aor. -έθανον, τέθνηκα, θανοῦμαι	to die, be dying
τιμάω, τιμήσω, ἐτίμησα, τετίμηκα, τετίμημαι, ἐτιμήθην	to honor
τεῖχος τείχους, τό	wall
ἴσως	equally, probably, perhaps
αἴρω, ἀρῶ, ἦρα, ἦρκα, ἦρμαι, ἤρθην	take up, lift up; remove
ἀποκτείνω, ἀποκτενῶ, ἀπέκτεινα, ἀπέκτονα	kill
στρατιώτης –ου, ὁ	soldier
ἄνευ	without (+gen.)
πότερος ποτέρα πότερον	which of the two? πότερον whether
ἁπλῶς	simply, plainly
πίπτω, πεσοῦμαι, ἔπεσον, πέπτωκα	fall, fall down
τέταρτος –η –ον	fourth

κατασκευάζω, κατασκευάσω, κατεσκεύασα	equip, furnish, make ready
ἐχθρός –ά –όν	hated, hateful; hostile to (+dat.)
ἀγών ἀγῶνος, ὁ	contest; struggle

401-450

κωλύω, κωλύσω, ἐκώλυσα, κεκώλυκα, κεκώλυμαι, ἐκωλύθην	hinder, check, prevent (+acc. and infin.)
ἁμαρτάνω, ἁμαρτήσομαι, ἡμάρτησα, 2 aor. ἥμαρτον, ἡμάρτηκα, ἡμάρτημαι, ἡμαρτήθην	miss the mark (+gen.); fail, be wrong, make a mistake
διαφθείρω, διαφθερῶ, διέφθειρα, διέφθαρκα, διέφθαρμαι, διεφθάρην	destroy; corrupt
πως	(enclitic) somehow, in some way, in any way
πόνος πόνου, ὁ	work, labor; stress, trouble, pain
ἔνθα	there
τάξις τάξεως, ἡ	arrangement, order; military unit
πειράω (usually mid. πειράομαι), πειράσομαι, ἐπείρασα, πεπείραμαι, ἐπειράθην	attempt, try, make a trial of (+gen.)
φοβέω, φοβήσω, ἐφόβησα, πεφόβημαι, ἐφοβήθην	put to flight; (mid. and pass.) flee, fear
βάλλω, βαλῶ, 2 aor. ἔβαλον, βέβληκα, βέβλημαι, ἐβλήθην	throw, hurl; throw at, hit (acc.) with (dat.)
πονηρός –ά –όν	worthless, bad, wicked
ξένος ξένου, ὁ	guest-friend; foreigner, stranger

βάρβαρος –ον	non-Greek, foreign; barbarous
ὅπου	where, wherever
συμφέρω, συνοίσω, 1 aor. συνήνεγκα	benefit, be useful or profitable to (+dat.); (impers.) συμφέρει it is of use, expedient (+infin.); τὸ συμφέρον use, profit, advantage
πυνθάνομαι, πεύσομαι, 2 aor. ἐπυθόμην, πέπυσμαι	learn, hear, inquire concerning (+gen.)
δοῦλος δούλου, ὁ	slave
τέμνω, τεμῶ, 2 aor. ἔτεμον, -τέτμηκα, τέτμημαι, ἐτμήθην	cut, cut down, cut to pieces
χρήσιμος χρησίμη χρήσιμον	useful, serviceable
ποῖος ποία ποῖον	what sort of?
ὅπλον ὅπλου, τό	weapon, tool, implement (mostly pl.)
πίστις πίστεως, ἡ	trust in others, faith; that which gives confidence, assurance, pledge, guarantee
ὑπολαμβάνω, ὑπολήψομαι, ὑπέλαβον, ὑπείληφα, ὑπείλημμαι, ὑπελήφθην	take up, seize; answer, reply; assume, suppose
ποιητής –οῦ, ὁ	creator, poet
λανθάνω, λήσω, ἔλαθον, λέληθα	escape the notice of (+acc. and nom. participle), be unknown; (mid. and pass.) forget
βελτίων βέλτιον	better (comp. of ἀγαθός)
πάντως	altogether, in all ways; at any rate
πορεύω, πορεύσω, ἐπόρευσα, πεπόρευμαι, ἐπορεύθην	carry; (mid. and pass) go, walk, march

ἀποκρίνω, ἀποκρινῶ, ἀπεκρινάμην, ἀπεκρίθη	separate, set apart; (mid.) answer, reply
πέντε	five
κίνδυνος κινδύνου, ὁ	danger
κατηγορέω, κατηγορήσω, κατηγόρησα, κατηγόρηκα, κατηγόρημαι, κατηγορήθην	to speak against, to accuse (+gen.)
τρέπω, τρέψω, ἔτρεψα, τέτροφα, ἐτράπην	turn, direct towards a thing; put to flight, defeat; (pass.) turn one's steps in a certain direction, go
ὅμως	nevertheless, all the same, notwithstanding
θεῖος θεία θεῖον	divine
ἱππεύς ἱππέως, ὁ	horseman, rider, charioteer
κτάομαι, κτήσομαι, ἐκτησάμην, κέκτημαι	get, gain, acquire
λείπω, λείψω, ἔλιπον, λέλοιπα, λέλειμμαι, ἐλείφθην	leave, abandon
βουλή βουλῆς, ἡ	will, determination; counsel, piece of advice; council of elders
ἐλπίς ἐλπίδος, ἡ	hope; expectation
γραφή γραφῆς, ἡ	a drawing, painting, writing; indictment
τίκτω, τέξω or τέξομαι, ἔτεκον, τέτοκα, τέτεγμαι, ἐτέχθην	beget, give birth to, produce
κομίζω, κομιῶ, ἐκόμισα, κεκόμικα, κεκόμισμαι, ἐκομίσθην	take care of, provide for
θυμός θυμοῦ, ὁ	life, spirit; soul, heart, mind

βλέπω, βλέψομαι, ἔβλεψα	see, look (at)
φόβος φόβου, ὁ	panic, fear, flight
πολιτεία –ας, ἡ	constitution, citizenship, republic
στάδιον σταδίου, τό (pl. στάδια and στάδιοι)	stadion or stade, the longest Greek unit of linear measure, about 185 meters
φρονέω, φρονήσω, ἐφρόνησα	think, intend to (+infin.); be minded towards (+adv. and dat.)
τοιόσδε τοιάδε τοιόνδε	such (as this), of such a sort (as this)

451-500

ὁρμάω, ὁρμήσω, ὥρμησα, ὥρμηκα, ὥρμημαι, ὡρμήθην	set in motion, urge on; (intrans.) start, hasten on
παρασκευάζω, παρασκευάσω, παρεσκεύασα	get ready, prepare, provide
λαλέω, λαλήσω, ἐλάλησα, λελάληκα, ἐλαλήθην	talk, chatter, babble
δράω, δράσω, ἔδρασα, δέδρακα, δέδραμαι, ἐδράσθην	do, accomplish
σκοπέω, σκοπήσω, ἐσκόπησα	look at, watch; look into, consider, examine
βοῦς βοός, ὁ/ἡ	bull, ox, cow
ἡμέτερος ἡμετέρα ἡμέτερον	our
γράμμα γράμματος, τό	letter, written character; (pl.) piece of writing, document(s)

ἐρωτάω, ἐρήσομαι, 2 aor. ἠρόμην	ask someone (acc.) something (acc.); question, beg
πολεμέω, πολεμήσω, ἐπολέμησα, πεπολέμηκα	make war
θύω, θύσω, ἔθυσα, τέθυκα, τέθυμαι, ἐτύθην	sacrifice
ἐλαύνω, ἐλῶ, ἤλασα, -ελήλακα, ἐλήλαμαι, ἠλάθην	drive, set in motion
δέδοικα, δείσομαι, ἔδεισα	fear
σύμμαχος –ον	allied with (+dat.); οἱ σύμμαχοι allies
ἡγεμών ἡγεμόνος, ὁ	guide, leader, commander
βαρύς βαρεῖα βαρύ	heavy, grievous, tiresome
ὧδε	thus, in this way; hither, here
αἰσχρός –ά –όν	ugly, shameful, disgraceful
εἰρήνη εἰρήνης, ἡ	peace
ἁλίσκομαι, ἁλώσομαι, 2 aor. ἑάλων, ἑάλωκα	to be taken, conquered (act. supplied by αἱρέω)
δέκα	ten
ἀμείνων ἄμεινον	better, abler, stronger, braver (comp. of ἀγαθός)
χείρων χεῖρον	worse, inferior (comp. of κακός)
βοηθέω, βοηθήσω, ἐβοήθησα, βεβοήθηκα	help, assist (+dat.)
λαμπρός –ά –όν	bright, brilliant; well-known, illustrious

ἀπαλλάσσω, ἀπαλλάξω, ἀπήλλαξα, ἀπήλλαχα, ἀπήλλαγμαι, ἀπηλλάχθην or ἀπηλλάγην	set free, release, deliver
βουλεύω βουλεύσω, ἐβούλευσα, βεβούλευκα, βεβούλευμαι, ἐβουλεύθην	plan (to), decide (to); (mid.) deliberate
μάλα	very, very much
αἰτέω, αἰτήσω, ᾔτησα, ᾔτηκα, ᾔτημαι, ᾐτήθην	ask (for), beg
σωτηρία σωτηρίας, ἡ	safety, deliverance
ἄρα	[introduces a question]
διώκω, διώξομαι, ἐδίωξα, δεδίωχα, ἐδιώχθην	pursue
δαίμων δαίμονος, ὁ/ἡ	spirit, god, demon
οὐκοῦν	surely then (inviting assent to an inference)
γλῶσσα γλώσσης, ἡ	tongue; language
ἑπτά	seven
τολμάω, τολμήσω, ἐτόλμησα, τετόλμηκα, τετόλμημαι, ἐτολμήθην	have the courage, dare; undertake, undergo
δεσπότης –ου, ὁ	master (of the household); absolute ruler
εἰκός εἰκότος, τό	likelihood, probability; εἰκός (ἐστι) it is likely (+infin.) →ἔοικα
ἄδικος ἄδικον	unjust
εἴκοσι(ν)	twenty

μυρίος μυρία μυρίον	countless; μύριοι 10,000; μυριάς -άδος ἡ 10,000, a countless amount
αὐτίκα	at once, immediately
δέκατος –η –ον	tenth
βαίνω, βήσομαι, 2 aor. ἔβην, βέβηκα	walk, come, go
περ	[enclitic added to pronouns and other particles for emphasis]
ἐλεύθερος ἐλευθέρα ἐλεύθερον	free, independent
στρατιά –ᾶς, ἡ	army
ἀμφί	about, around
συμφορά –ᾶς, ἡ	event, circumstance, misfortune

501-519

ἑκατόν	hundred
νίκη νίκης, ἡ	victory
ἔπος ἔπους, τό	word, speech, tale; prophecy
στρατός –οῦ, ὁ	army
φράζω, φράσω, ἔφρασα, πέφρακα, πέφρασμαι, ἐφράσθην	tell, declare; (mid. and pass.) think (about)
ἀργύριον ἀργυρίου, τό	money
τριάκοντα	thirty
ἕξ	six
πεμπτός –ή –όν	fifth
μάρτυς μάρτυρος, ὁ/ἡ	witness

GREEK: Frequency Listing

χαλκοῦς –ῆ –οῦν	of copper or bronze
ἕβδομος –η –ον	seventh
ποῦ	where
ναί	indeed, yes (used in strong affirmation)
φῶς φωτός, τό	light, daylight
ὀκτώ	eight
ἕκτος –η –ον	sixth
τριακοστός –ή –όν	thirtieth
ἐννέα	nine
πότε	when?
ὄγδοος –η –ον	eighth
ἔνατος –α –ον	ninth
εἰκοστός –ή –όν	twentieth
ἀγγέλλω, ἀγγελῶ, ἤγγειλα, ἤγγελκα, ἤγγελμαι, ἠγγέλθην	report, tell
ἑκατοστός –ή –όν	hundredth

CPSIA information can be obtained
at www.ICGtesting.com
Printed in the USA
LVHW080308260621
691221LV00002B/191

9 781947 822061